LEARNING
SUPPORT UNITS

LEARNING SUPPORT UNITS

Principles, Practice and Evaluation

Jane McSherry

David Fulton Publishers

David Fulton Publishers Ltd
The Chiswick Centre, 414 Chiswick High Road, London W4 5TF

www.fultonpublishers.co.uk

First published in Great Britain in 2004 by David Fulton Publishers

10 9 8 7 6 5 4 3 2 1

Note: The right of the author to be identified as the author of this work has been
asserted by her in accordance with the Copyright, Designs and Patents Act 1988.

David Fulton Publishers is a division of Granada Learning Limited, part of ITV plc.

Copyright © Jane McSherry 2004

British Library Cataloguing in Publication Data
A catalogue record for this book is available from the British Library.

ISBN 1 84312 061 5

Typeset by RefineCatch Limited, Bungay, Suffolk
Printed and bound in Great Britain

Contents

Acknowledgements

Thanks are due to colleagues around the country who run LSUs. I have written this book for you and with the help of many of you.

Special thanks go to colleagues in Wandsworth schools and support services, with whom it is my great pleasure to work on a day-to-day basis.

A debt of gratitude is owed to colleagues who have written case studies and who have offered support and insights in the preparation of this manuscript: Saul Becker, Leora Cruddas, Terry Debney, Barbara Hopgood, Catherine Lloyd, Sarah Norris, Viv McCrossen, Miriam Oakley, Nicola Stanfield, Penelope Stephen and Yvette Unsworth.

My heartfelt love and thanks go to my father, Professor Duncan Harris, who for many years has been my mentor, proof reader and idea generator, and without whom this book would never have been finished. He has given of his time, support and love without question or limit.

And last but not least to my husband and my children, who have been patient and quiet for too many weekends.

Dedication

For my grandfather, the Reverend Wilfred Georgeson (1906–2003), who admired and supported the pursuit of knowledge. I'm sorry you didn't get to share the elation at the completion of my PhD but I know you were there in spirit. This book is dedicated to you by way of thanks for your love and belief in me.

Introduction

Key themes

There are some key themes that run through this book and are explored in different chapters and illustrated through the different stages and processes of developing a Learning Support Unit (LSU). One of these themes is a whole school approach to managing and supporting pupils with challenging behaviours. To be effective the LSU needs to be part of a whole school approach. Ways of promoting and developing this idea are illustrated throughout the book. One part of this process is communication. Practical ways of ensuring that communicating and negotiating are at the forefront of LSU plans and implementation are highlighted.

A second theme is changing pupil behaviour through the development of more effective strategies for dealing with school life and helping them learn to learn. LSU programmes need to offer a curriculum which reflects the academic as well as the social and emotional needs of the pupils referred for support.

A third key theme is working with colleagues to promote changes in teacher behaviour, as part of continued professional development. The LSU has a role in supporting teaching staff in providing an appropriate learning environment for pupils that responds to their particular needs. This support will include working with colleagues, and exploring together strategies that work and different ways of enhancing the learning experience for all pupils.

How to use this book

The book may be used differently by people in different roles and at various stages in the development of the LSU.

- The manager of an established LSU may want to start by reading the chapter on reporting, evaluation, monitoring and recording (Chapter 6) because this may be an area identified for development within his/her school.

- A school starting to think through the process of implementing such an initiative may want to work through the chapters in the existing order. There is intended to be a logical progression through the chapters for colleagues new to the process. They may also want to work through Appendix 5, which outlines specific areas to consider when setting up a new LSU.

- Members of an in-school steering group may wish to reflect on information in Appendix 5 and, depending on the stage of development of the LSU, highlight areas in Chapters 3 to 6 for discussion and review. For example, if the steering group is discussing exit and entry criteria, Chapter 4 could be a starting point for discussion and collaborative problem-solving.

- New LSU managers may want to start with Chapter 3, which explores the role of the LSU manager, and use this as a basis for discussion with senior management about whole school approaches.

- LEA staff new to the role of supporting LSU staff may wish to read Chapter 7 first, which considers ways of supporting LSU managers. They may also wish to consider promoting a steering group model as discussed in Appendix 5, or a referral panel model as illustrated in Chapter 4.

How the chapters are laid out

Chapters explore a specific area such as the role of the LSU manager, entry and exit criteria, etc. Information in the chapters is designed to be for consideration by new LSU managers, and for review and reflection by managers of more established LSUs and other teachers within the school reflecting on their practice. Each chapter starts with a list of questions that the chapter aims to address. Areas are then explored with the aid of case-study examples. Each chapter ends with some conclusions and there are then suggestions for taking ideas forward. These suggestions could be used as the basis for discussion and perhaps training activities, either within schools or at LEA network sessions.

Case studies illustrating good practice

There are case-study illustrations in each chapter which are intended to present interesting and innovative practice from LSUs in a variety of LEAs across the country. Some of these LSUs are Excellence in Cities (EiC) funded and others are not. Some are funded through other government initiatives and others through the schools' own resources. The issues for colleagues in running these units are the same, as are the concerns about continued funding in the short and medium term. I have highlighted, where appropriate, where DfES guidance or documents have been issued reflecting on the LSU initiative. These documents should not be taken as the only way to run an LSU, and they vary in their usefulness. However, as there is a dearth of information and reflection on the work of LSUs, consideration of all existing literature is prudent.

Summary of chapter contents

Chapter 1 offers an overview of the LSU initiative and may be of interest to anyone who is not familiar with the development of thinking behind the current DfES model. This is the most frequently asked for element of initial training that I deliver and is usually my starting point in prompting thinking for LSU managers. This does not imply that the DfES model is the only model, but just that as a starting point for understanding some of the developments in thinking the research exploring successful elements of previous projects is useful. Chapter 1 also briefly summarises Ofsted findings about the LSU initiative and what an inspection may expect to see in the LSU.

Chapter 2 explores a whole school audit/review process and explains why this is important. For schools implementing a new initiative, using an audit process prior to starting ensures that the LSU is part of a whole school strategy and complements existing support. Schools with an existing LSU can use the process to review the implementation of the LSU as part of the whole school system to address behaviour issues. The chapter uses an illustrative case study to explore an audit, implementation, monitoring and evaluation cycle.

Chapter 3 explores the role of the LSU manager and how that is defined and communicated within the school. The role has various functions, including:

- assessing pupils' needs, and planning appropriate programmes of intervention
- communicating with other staff about pupils and their needs
- promoting the LSU as a whole school initiative
- influencing the practice of other staff
- providing training and support to other staff
- developing and maintaining links with other agencies
- developing and maintaining links to the Pastoral Support Programme (PSP) process.

Each of these aspects will be explored within the chapter.

Chapter 4 looks at entry and exit criteria and strategies for successful re-integration of pupils after the intervention. The chapter explores the importance of developing clear entry criteria and effective referral procedures, including the use of in-school referral panels. Pupil involvement in the process is highlighted throughout. This chapter also explores the need to clarify exit criteria and uses some specific examples of innovative practice to illustrate possible re-integration strategies.

Chapter 5 looks at programmes within the LSU and highlights the need to look in a holistic way at the support pupils may need to help them achieve their potential within a mainstream school environment. Programmes will need to reflect both a social, emotional and academic curriculum.

Chapter 6 looks at recording, reporting, monitoring and evaluating the work of the LSU. A planned approach to undertaking these tasks is recommended, and consideration is given to the different audiences that may need to access this information.

Chapter 7 explores the important role the LEA plays in providing advice, support and training for schools in the implementation of the LSU initiatives. It also looks at how networks for LSU managers can be set up and maintained. The activities an LEA can co-ordinate will vary, but some examples explored in this chapter include the setting up and co-ordination of an LEA-wide database, specific training for LSU managers, helping schools across an LEA with the primary–secondary transfer process and regular network sessions for LSU managers to share good practice and facilitate the dissemination of up-to-date information relevant to managers and schools implementing the initiative.

In addition, Appendix 5 includes advice and areas for consideration when planning a new LSU. It includes separate sections on:

- Establishing a steering group for the LSU
- Locating the unit within the school
- The learning environment
- Staffing
- Discipline
- Linked Units

These sections are designed to be considered separately by a working group planning the implementation of the LSU.

Other appendices included proformas and additional information from chapters within the book.

Overview of the LSU initiative

- *How have recent projects influenced the DfES guidelines for the LSU initiative?*

- *What relevant research has been carried out, i.e. Evaluation of the Behaviour and Discipline Pilot Projects (Hallam and Castle 1999)?*

- *What are the good practice indicators?*

- *How are expectations of the initiative changing and developing?*

- *What has Ofsted reported about the initiative?*

- *What is the purpose of an LSU?*

Introduction

There is some debate about the use of the term 'Learning Support Units' and, more particularly, with the word 'unit'. I have used this term as it is the most commonly used term to describe this type of in-school provision.

The chapter will introduce the key elements to be expanded in subsequent chapters. The content is based on INSET materials that I have used in many local authorities. An overview of the LSU initiative and the thinking behind the DfES model are frequently requested, which seems to indicate that these may have been missed by many practitioners involved in delivering the LSU initiative.

The framework for the LSU initiative

Some key issues on providing effective practice for pupils with emotional and behavioural difficulties in mainstream schools were raised in a research report published in 1998 (Daniels *et al.* 1998). Many of the points raised reinforced those skills and policies needed for developing effective practice for all pupils in an inclusive school:

- *Leadership:* Head teachers and senior management teams who provide effective leadership, particularly in communicating the appropriate values, ethos and aspirations of the school.

- *Sharing values:* A core of staff who work together to promote the values of the school, working with all pupils in ensuring these values and aspirations are realised in practice.

- *Behaviour policy and practice:* A consistent and well-monitored behaviour policy where the approaches taken with pupils with emotional and behavioural difficulties are an extension of behaviour policy for all pupils.

- *Understanding EBD:* Key members of staff who understand the nature of emotional and behavioural difficulties, and are able to distinguish these from sporadic misbehaviour or short-term emotional difficulties.

- *Teaching skills and the curriculum:* Effective teaching skills for pupils with EBD are the same as those for all pupils, including the ability to learn from one's own actions, and teaching an appropriately challenging curriculum.

What the research highlighted was the need for whole school approaches when dealing with pupils with emotional and behavioural difficulties. The PACE project, which ran from 1996–7 (Cooper *et al.* 2000), took a different perspective, being particularly interested in the views of pupils. This research offered some valuable evidence about the impact of school ethos and individual teacher attitudes to pupils, and the effect this had on how pupils perceive themselves and their worth. The underlying assumption of this research was that solutions lay in being able to listen to and learn from the perspectives of others.

Good practice in developing in-school centres was summarised in the Evaluation of the Behaviour and Discipline Pilot Projects (Hallam and Castle 1999). The DfEE used the outcomes of this research to develop guidance in *Social Inclusion: Pupil Support* (circular 10/99) (DfEE 1999a) and also in the *Excellence in Cities* document (DfEE 1999b). It is worth, therefore, looking at the projects evaluated in this research in more detail to understand the context of the aims and promotion of in-school centres (LSUs).

LEAs bid for the opportunity to participate in the Behaviour and Discipline Pilot Projects, which were Standards Fund projects. There were three different types of projects available under this funding: multi-disciplinary behaviour support teams; in-school centres; and the secondment of teachers from mainstream schools to Pupil Referral Units (PRUs).

> The overall aim of the projects was to make fundamental changes to the way that schools perceived and managed children at risk leading to changes in practice which would be maintained in the long term.
> (Hallam and Castle 1999: 6)

The idea of an in-school unit within this model was therefore not a 'sin bin', a place to send disruptive pupils to get them out of everyone's way. It was about a strategy that was designed to make a difference in the long term to professional practice within the school as a whole, not just within the unit.

The evaluation of the in-school centre strand of the Behaviour and Discipline Pilot Projects indicated that although there was wide variation in the degree of success, the centres were, overall, successful in reducing permanent exclusions (Hallam and Castle 1999). Further, the evaluation team concluded that there were some specific factors that contributed to the success of the in-school centres:

- The active involvement of senior staff, teachers and parents
- Good communication within the school
- Using an approach which combined the withdrawal of pupils and support for them within normal classes
- Flexibility in the provision of support
- The involvement of pupils in self-monitoring

Hallam and Castle's report offers examples of good practice on a range of aspects of the work of an in-school centre.

Building on the success of the Behaviour and Discipline Pilot Projects, the DfEE extended the funding for the implementation of the in-school centre initiative, now called Learning Support Units, to the Excellence in Cities areas. Guidance for the implementation of the LSU strand was detailed in guidance that went to all schools in circular 10/99 (DfEE 1999a).

Social Inclusion: Pupil Support (10/99) (DfEE 1999a) summarises Learning Support Units as

- a positive preventative strategy
- needing clear entry and exit criteria including time limits of up to two terms on pupils' attendance
- providing a planned entry rather than instant referral
- providing separate short-term teaching and support programmes tailored to the needs of difficult pupils
- school-based – sometimes shared
- enabling pupils to manage in the mainstream classroom and therefore setting relevant activities, such as individual targets, anger management and social skills courses; targeted numeracy and literacy work may be included
- providing an appropriate curriculum with teachers and centre staff liaising over setting and marking relevant work.

There is a clear implication within these points that units are not about minding pupils whilst they complete their class work but about a structured and planned intervention, with full re-integration as the aim.

When LEAs were invited to bid for funding for LSUs from Excellence in Cities the guidelines indicated the desired outcomes of an LSU initiative, and included:

- evidence of improvements, likely to be long lasting, that have been made at a whole school systems' level
- substantial and potentially long-lasting improvements in behaviour and attainment of individual pupils supported by the project
- improvements that are likely to be long lasting in staff approaches to pupil behaviour and assessment processes and procedures, for example working with parents.

These outcomes clearly indicate work on three levels: individual pupils; staff approaches throughout the school; and changes to school systems. The emphasis reflects work at a whole school level, with teachers being supported in developing their professional practice and pupils improving both behaviour and learning. The guidance further indicated that LSUs should model key elements for the successful teaching of troubled and troublesome pupils, and these included:

- small teaching groups
- a good relationship with a teacher
- ready access to teacher assistance with work
- accurately differentiated work
- pupils listened to and their opinions valued
- disruptive behaviour being coped with and worked with.

How expectations of the initiative are changing and developing

As indicated in the Introduction, there are LSUs across the country funded in a variety of ways and using a variety of models. There has yet to be a national training programme, although one has been promised for a number of years. The Excellence in

Cities (EiC) initiative has been evaluated more widely because it involves huge sums of money and is a specific government focus. Other LSUs have not been considered in the same way because they are part of school or LEA initiatives. There is no implication in this book that LSUs developed in EiC areas are following the 'right' model (the case studies in this book are taken from EiC and non-EiC areas), but it is worth reflecting on the documentation of good practice in these areas as it is more readily available. For example, as a result of the experience in a number of Phase 1 EiC areas, *Good Practice Guidelines* were issued in 2002 to all registered LSUs. These guidelines were devised from talking to LSU managers, visiting schools and exploring what worked in practice. The guidelines indicated that an LSU intervention needed to:

- be short-term
- be aimed at re-integration
- be for a targeted cohort of pupils
- devise and deliver individual packages
- assist primary–secondary transition
- be flexible.

Devising and delivering individual packages has been emphasised over the last few years and clearly moves from a model of 'minding' pupils to one of active intervention. Using LSUs to assist in the transition from primary schools to secondary schools is a new and interesting development (this will be further explored in Chapter 7).

Other points raised within these guidelines were that to be successful there needed to be a whole school understanding of the role and function of the LSU, with effective communication. A suggestion to enhance communication was the development of a Social Inclusion Team and an audit of existing systems and structures. At a local authority level there was a clearly indicated need for training and support of LSU managers. All of these suggestions would be of value to LSU managers in their roles whatever way their unit was funded.

Ofsted evaluation of new initiatives

A recent evaluation of the management and impact of Excellence in Cities and Education Action Zones (Ofsted 2003) offers some important clarification on what Ofsted considers to be good practice in LSU provision. You can access the document directly on the Internet at www.ofsted.gov/publications/docs/1031.pdf but you will need Acrobat Reader on your computer to download the document. The common features of successful LSU provision cited within this document include:

- Well organised learning environments
- Thorough assessment of pupils
- Varied programmes of activities
- Clear entry and exit criteria
- Continued attendance at successful lessons
- Liaison between unit manager, class teachers, tutors, year head and parents, and with outside agencies.

Ofsted also highlighted some specific issues that are vitally important if we are considering both the interventions that we are providing and the process by which we will evaluate if they are working.

According to the report, 'While providing good care and personal support, a quarter of learning support units did not do enough to help pupils learn more effectively' (Ofsted 2003: 58). Given that many pupils referred for support in LSUs do have additional learning difficulties, in order to aid their re-integration in the short term, or their success in the long term, the LSU needs to address their learning needs as well as their emotional and behavioural needs.

The counter point to this is that LSUs set up to provide a location where pupils complete the work they have been set in previous lessons are seen to be offering little more that a pupil-minding service. Pupils from various lessons completing work set by someone else often have little opportunity to work as a group or develop important social and learning skills that are needed for more successful school life. Opportunities to develop both social and learning skills in a balance of activities is important. Many of the pupils referred to the LSU will need support with developing strategies for learning, socialising and working with others. Being able to work as a group and develop mutually supportive peer relations within the LSU can have positive effects across their school life for pupils. Many units are offering intensive work on basic literacy and numeracy for pupils within a group-working context. LSU programmes will be explored in more detail in Chapter 5.

A further point made by the Ofsted evaluation was that procedures for entry and exit need to be clear. It is worth stressing the point that if we do have clear entry and exit criteria and baseline data, we can provide the most effective programmes for pupils and evaluate whether what we are offering is working. The evaluation by Ofsted cited monitoring and evaluation as a general weakness of LSUs.

> Systematic monitoring and evaluation were the weakest feature of most learning support units. Few schools could demonstrate objectively the effectiveness of the unit or identify the most successful approaches for pupils of different age groups.   (Ofsted 2003: 60)

This issue is considered in Chapter 6 and some strategies suggested.

To summarise, key aspects of a successful LSU are:

Pupils

- Well organised learning environments
- Thorough assessment of pupils
- Varied programmes of activities
- Help for pupils to learn more effectively.

Systems

- Clear entry and exit criteria
- Continued attendance at successful lessons
- Liaison between unit manager, class teachers, tutors, year head and parents, and with outside agencies
- Systematic monitoring and evaluation.

What is the purpose of a Learning Support Unit?

If you ask LSU managers what the purpose of the LSU is, you get a wide variety of responses – some dependent on the way the unit works in their schools and some on how they would like it to work. There is usually a high level of consensus that an LSU can be many things. What is important is to be clear what the LSU is and what it is not.

When LSU managers in a training session were asked the question '*What are the aims of the LSU?*' they gave a range of responses, listed below in Box 1.1. The same question posed in other training sessions has elicited a similar variety of responses.

Box 1.1	Reponses given by LSU managers to the question 'What are the aims of the LSU?'

Preventing exclusions
Mid-phase transfers (KS 3–4)
Transition work for Year 7s

Re-integration
Provide specialist programmes but also to keep mainstream focus
Short-term intervention
Challenge schools to have inclusive focus
Raise levels of achievement

Challenge teachers
Give teachers a break
Building links with parents

Challenge pupils' ideas
Enabling
Spread ideas and promote good practice

Some schools have decided to use a 'virtual' LSU model where there is no location as such, but the work of supporting and including pupils is done in and around the school by LSU staff. It is a model that can be open to problems, for example, LSU staff can end up patrolling the corridors for pupils who are out of lessons and trying to persuade them back in. On the other hand it can work well and is seen by some schools as the answer to their problems. Barrow *et al.* (2001) see virtual LSUs as a concept rather than LSUs with no location. They suggest that a virtual LSU is at one end of a continuum, the opposite end being a 'fixed unit'. A fixed unit in this context, they suggest, is one which develops its own policies, has little intention of re-integrating pupils and which operates in isolation from the rest of the school. Clearly, as with most extremes, either end of the continuum has specific and perhaps irreconcilable problems. A unit which takes the best aspects of both extremes, and moulds them into a process which meets the needs of the individual school and its pupils, is likely to be the most successful type of provision.

It is important to clarify from the outset that whatever source of funding has been used or is being used to implement the LSU within your context, the LSU initiative sits within wider social inclusion strategies. These include a range of strategies, such as:

- Learning Mentors
- Pastoral Support Programmes (PSPs)
- Connexions, Personal Advisers (PAs)
- Behaviour Improvement Programmes (BIP) within the Excellence in Cities (EiC) areas.

These strategies are influenced by and complementary to more all-embracing inclusion strategies for pupils with all kinds of special needs, including the new Code of Practice and the Disability legislation. For the LSU to have the greatest impact on school policies and practice, as well as on the improvement of the potential and possibilities for individual pupils, it must be part of a clearly planned raft of possible interventions and strategies within a school. The LSU manager and team need to be valued and actively supported in their work by the school senior management team and, by extension, the staff as a whole. The rest of this book will offer advice and strategies on how to achieve these aims.

Conclusions

The LSU should enhance existing structures and be part of a whole school strategy for supporting vulnerable pupils. One way of ensuring this is the practice of the school from the outset is to undertake an audit/review of existing support and structures prior to the implementation of a new strategy.

The LSU needs to support and change the behaviour both of pupils and of staff if the impact is to be at a whole school level. The opportunity to work with other staff and offer professional support and development is part of the work of the LSU manager.

There need to be well established and clear entry and exit criteria through a referral process. Re-integration is the fundamental aim of the LSU initiative and needs to be planned and supported.

Programmes within the LSU need to reflect the needs of the pupils academically, socially and emotionally. Pupils should be actively involved at each stage of the process.

Planned monitoring and evaluation of the initiative are vital. It is only by effectively monitoring and evaluating the programmes and progress towards the aims of the initiative that it can be developed to meet the needs of the pupils and staff within the school most effectively.

The LEA has an important role to play in supporting and training LSU managers.

Suggestions for taking ideas forward

Exploring some of the research papers presented here in more detail may promote discussion and ideas at either a school or LEA-network level. The recognition that the LSU manager's role is wider that pupil management is a vital component in promoting an effective whole school initiative.

Some questions that could be considered for discussion are:

■ How is the work of the LSU promoted within the school?

■ Is there a need for a discussion with representatives of the whole school community (teachers, pupils, parents/carers, lunchtime supervisors, etc.) to reflect on the purposes of the LSU?

■ How will the LSU affect the professional development of teachers within the school?

■ Is the programme (or planned programme) within the LSU covering pupils' social, emotional and academic needs?

■ What changes in practice for the whole school are necessary to make the LSU more effective?

2 Changing school systems to improve pupil behaviour

- *Why is a whole school audit/review an important process?*

- *What are the stages in a review and planning cycle?*

- *How is an auditing, implementing, monitoring and evaluating cycle carried out?*

Introduction

New initiatives

Over the last three to five years many new initiatives specifically designed to assist schools with additional strategies for improving pupils' behaviour have been introduced. Some examples of these are (and you will be able to think of many more):

- Learning Mentors
- Learning Support Units
- Pastoral Support Programmes
- Connexions
- Behaviour Improvement Programmes
- New Code of Practice
- Disability legislation

Many schools report that they feel as if they have barely understood the implications of one initiative before another is introduced. Yet if these initiatives are to be effective they require changes to the school system, and if initiatives come in a steady stream schools need constantly to address the question of system change. It is a problem because these types of initiatives cannot be fully implemented except as part of a whole school approach, and in order to be part of a whole school approach changes to the existing systems in a school will be necessary.

This chapter will explore the wider school systems that need to be reviewed before implementing the LSU initiative. This process is equally valid as an ongoing review and change cycle for schools with existing LSUs, or where problems have arisen with the implementation of any aspect of the continuum of support for behaviour.

Evidence-based practice

Using the evidence of what works well and where the gaps in provision exist, schools can effectively plan for changes and additional resources. A staged approach to reviewing existing practice and making necessary adjustments is needed in order to

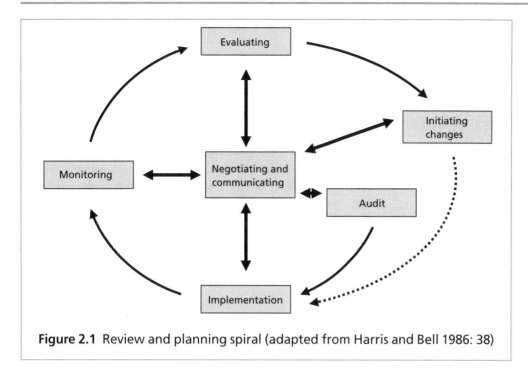

Figure 2.1 Review and planning spiral (adapted from Harris and Bell 1986: 38)

foster improvement at the personal and the systems level. It is important that staff see themselves as stakeholders in the process of change, rather than as recipients of constant edicts.

There are four key stages to this process:

1 Audit/reviewing

2 Implementing

3 Monitoring

4 Evaluating

Negotiating and communicating is central to each stage of this process, as illustrated in Figure 2.1.

Audit/review

An audit or review allows us to look at what is working in the present situation and, importantly, what is not. Some people are unhappy with the term 'audit' (and recently schools' staff have been asked to complete a number of audits). However, whether we use the term 'audit' or 'review' the process is still the same. The term audit will be used to describe the process illustrated in this section. This process allows changes to systems to be planned and based on the evidence provided by the audit. Audits are a useful starting point for reviewing existing practice. The DfES has promoted several recently, including the *Index for Inclusion* (CSIE 2000), QCA Behaviour Scales for whole school planning, a recent audit tool for Learning Support Units (DfES 2002b) and various audit tools for the Learning Mentor initiative (DfES 2002d).

Some of the most effective changes to the way systems work started with an audit. An example of a successful audit process undertaken in a school is included in the case study in the following sections.

Reviewing existing systems to identify needs

The first element of the process is to clarify the purpose of the audit and its main objectives. This decision will influence who needs to be included and what sort of questions should be asked. Clearly if the aim of the audit is to try to find out why communication with parents seems to be patchy, initial consultations will need to be with parents, staff and pupils. If, however, a review of internal processes for behaviour management is required the place to start is by consulting staff. Using the data collected from this first stage, decisions can be made on whom to include in a further stage of the audit. It is important to make the task manageable and thinking of it in stages is often helpful. If the initial plan is to consult with everyone who has any contact with the school the task can become enormous, unstructured and probably unstarted!

So the first question should be:

What is the purpose of the audit and what are the main objectives of conducting it?

The next question is about who we need to include in the first stage. There could also be proposals for the next stage and who might need to be included in this.

Who might we need to consult?

- Colleagues

- Parents

- Pupils

- Other professionals

- Other services

Having decided why we are using an audit and what we hope to gain by the process, and having identified whose views need to be sought, the next planning stage involves the questions to which we need answers. Below are some examples of questions we might ask in relation to planning a new (or reviewing an existing) LSU. These questions will be different for each institution and will depend on the stage at which they are.

What do we need to know about:

Users?

- What are users happy with?

- What are users unhappy with?

The system?

- How would the system work ideally?

- What are the constraints?

- Can any of the constraints be overcome?

- How does the system work at the moment?

- Who is involved in it?

Starting the process

All those involved in the present system should be represented in the review and planning cycle. The process may best be explained through the use of case study material. The case study used to illustrate the process being described has been chosen because it is an example of a successful audit process and, in addition, one of the three key issues identified and changed through the planning process was the Learning Support Unit.

Part One of the case study (below) gives some background information and describes the process used for the audit stage. The school invited an LEA support team to undertake the audit process – the team consisted of teachers and educational psychologists. The aim of the audit was to look at existing school systems with the views of all staff taken into account. The LEA support team were involved in both gathering the information and facilitating a dialogue amongst school staff.

When starting an audit process it is important to be clear about the questions/issues that the review needs to address. Asking for assistance from outside the school with gathering this information was a deliberate way of emphasising the importance given to the review and also allowed all staff to express views, in confidence, to someone outside the system. There is no suggestion that this process cannot be conducted internally, but it is often beneficial to involve outside professionals.

Evidence-based system change: case study, part one

The school senior management team (SMT) were concerned about the rising numbers of exclusions in the school and the way that some teachers were sending pupils out of their classes and straight to the Head, by-passing any departmental or year group systems. This was leading to a lack of consistency in the application of the school's behaviour policy and system of sanctions and rewards. The SMT asked for help from the LEA support service to conduct an audit, work with the staff of the school over a year, promote constructive discussion about behaviour and develop an agreed system of response to challenging behaviour.

Audit

Questionnaires

All staff were given a questionnaire (this was adapted from one suggested by Hill and Parsons (2000)). The questionnaire explored staff perceptions about various aspects of the whole school behaviour policy, including the policy itself, rewards and sanctions, roles and responsibilities, pupil behaviour, parental consultation, break time and lunch time, supervision outside the classroom and conflict resolution. The questionnaires were introduced at a morning briefing by the Head. It was made clear that everyone's views were being sought, that questionnaires remained anonymous and that the LEA team would be analysing the results. Completed questionnaires were placed in an envelope in the school office and collected on a specified date by a member of the LEA team.

Interviews

In addition to the questionnaires a third of the staff group were interviewed by a member of the project team. The only specific selection criterion was that there needed to be mixture of target groups: newly qualified teachers, staff new to the school, established staff, senior staff, support staff, etc. Interview responses were anonymous but grouped according to the target group status (questions asked in the staff interviews are included in Appendix 1). The analysis could thus reflect if certain issues were different for different groups and would therefore help in developing an appropriate action plan.

Classroom observations

Classroom observations were undertaken to compare how different teachers managed behaviour and to survey the level of consistency around the school. This information was gathered to inform the revision of the behaviour policy rather than to 'criticise' or 'praise' individual staff or departments. The observations concentrated on arrival to lessons, routines and strategies used by staff.

This case study illustrates a variety of ways of gathering information. Different types of information gathering will elicit varying levels of response. For example, response to the questionnaires gave a flavour for the consensus of responses across the whole staff group. It was clearly able to show some shared concerns as well as some more individual responses. The interviews asked for information in more detail about individual teacher responses to the system, and also about the strategies used by individual teachers. From this it was possible to start to see where there were shared strategies and how staff felt supported in dealing with problem behaviours. It highlighted where there was likely to be confusion for pupils and where there was consistency and clarity. The observations gave a snapshot of life for a pupil around the school.

Implementing change

Having identified areas of strength and areas of concern and developed an action plan, the next phase is implementing the changes identified through this process. Some key points to bear in mind when implementing change are:

- *Communication is vital* – having asked others for information it is important that we communicate thanks for their involvement, how the information they provided was used and what the proposals for action are at this stage. In the case study example the whole staff group were involved in the action plan development; however, this is often not the case, so informing everyone of the proposals is vital.

- *Pace the change* – making too many changes at once tends to unsettle everyone and make it very difficult to evaluate which change was effective and which irrelevant.

- *Ask for feedback on new systems* – having made changes it is important to monitor how they are working, if they are effective and why they are effective. It is important to canvass views about what is better and why.

- *Monitor the feedback* – if feedback is suggesting that the changes are a disaster for clear reasons it is important to use this information to further refine the changes.

- *Flexibility of response is important* – if it is clear that the changes are not working, rethink sooner rather than later. Persisting with something that is making things worse or causing concern is unhelpful. However a caveat may be that sometimes things do get worse before they get better, so your constructive feedback and monitoring process should be part of any decision to abandon changes.

- *Whole school participation* – everyone needs to know what is different and how the new system will work. Monitoring effectiveness is difficult if only half the staff are implementing it and the pupils are unclear about the change (or, worse, still blissfully ignorant!). If you have involved all the staff and communicated with them the how and why of any proposed changes they will, hopefully, have ownership of the process and will participate in a positive way. Involving pupils and enabling them to feel ownership of the process too has obvious further benefits.

The second part of the review and planning cycle illustrated in Figure 2.1 was now completed. Within this model it was communicated and negotiated with all those involved. This communication and negotiation is an essential part of involving all the stakeholders in changing school systems.

Feedback to the whole staff group

Key findings

Policy

■ Policy in place but inconsistently applied

■ Policy needed revising

SMT role

■ Staff felt unsupported by SMT and unclear about the role of SMT within the framework for challenging behaviour

Lesson changes

■ There were some problem 'hot spots', especially around lesson change-overs

■ Lateness to lessons was a problem and was inconsistently handled

■ There were widely varying routines for arrival at and the beginning of lessons

Behaviour expectations

■ There was little positive praise 'catching them being good'

■ There was not a clear link between rules, consequences and a hierarchy of sanctions

LSU

■ There was a lack of clarity about the purpose of the LSU, what happened there and how pupils were accepted for support

The initial staff feedback and planning session took place on a half day's in-service training. The LEA team fed back key findings from the audit and facilitated sessions throughout the morning, looking at various changes needed and developing an agreed action plan for priorities.

Some of the problem areas identified needed further analysis, for example, lesson change-over had been identified as an area of potential problems with some areas of the site being identified as 'hot spots'. It was agreed from this feedback and planning session that a member of the LEA team would work with a sub-group of staff to observe and monitor these hot spots and change-overs generally and report back to the whole staff group on proposals for change.

Changes were needed in the use of rewards and sanctions. For example, there seemed little uniformity among staff in the use of rewards. In addition, the rewards were felt to work for Key Stage 3 (KS3) but be less effective or relevant for Key Stage 4 (KS4). A sub-group of the staff agreed to work on proposals for a systematic use of rewards and sanctions for the school.

A further area for development was the LSU. Many staff were unclear about the referral process, entry and exit criteria and what the programme in the LSU consisted of. Time was allocated for the manager to talk to the whole staff over a series of meetings about the LSU. In addition, a referral panel model was discussed where all referrals for support would be considered by a panel of staff and appropriate support planned for individual pupils. This panel would also develop feedback systems so that staff referring pupils knew what support was being offered to them.

(continued)

Issues identified for action by the staff

■ Punctuality to lessons and the need to reduce travel time between lessons

■ Consistent routines for classroom entry, registration, gaining attention and class dismissal

■ Linking rules with consequences and a hierarchy of sanctions

■ Training in positive behaviour management

■ Support for struggling students and peer support for staff

■ Clarify the referral criteria and exit procedures from the LSU

Monitoring the actions proposed

Monitoring any change in an agreed timeframe is important so that everyone involved is still able to contribute to the process. It also allows for fine tuning of the changes taking place. In the case study example most of the staff were involved in one of the proposed actions and there were regular updates in staff meetings on the sub-groups following each action. If the whole staff group is not involved in the changes it is important regularly to seek people's perceptions about the changes or progress on changes. Having decided on a timeframe for review it is also helpful to decide what is being monitored, how it is being monitored, when it is being monitored and who will be gathering the information. For the school in the case study example, by dividing the tasks into sub-groups there was an expectation that each sub-group would decide on what information to gather and how to do this. With everyone involved in some aspect of the process, ownership is retained after the initial audit process.

Evidence-based system change: case study, part three

Responses to initial changes and proposals for further action: follow-up meeting with the whole staff group

After one term the whole staff group met with the project team for a further half day's in-service training to look at the progress made and to develop an action plan for the next steps.

The feedback from the observations and proposals for changes at lesson change-overs had resulted in an agreement for quite radical change. It was decided to completely revamp the timetable to take into account the split site effect of the two main teaching blocks. These two teaching blocks were joined by one route that was an area of conflict and problems at lesson change-over. Part of the problem was the sheer numbers of pupils going in two directions and all trying to get to lessons before they were late. The route became difficult to supervise because of the numbers of pupils. A suggested solution was the minimising of change-overs that required movement from one block to the other. Lessons would, wherever possible, be timetabled for teaching groups within one block, with movement to the other block taking place after a break. By minimising the number of pupils having to move between lessons from one block to the other it was hoped that the trouble 'hot spot' would diminish. It was agreed to implement this change as soon as the timetable could be changed, and a limit of a month was set on this.

The rewards were still an area of difficulty as the system and the rewards needed to be whole school but with adaptations at KS4. Further discussion was facilitated at this meeting and a system of merit slips agreed, where a certain number of merits could be exchanged for a voucher. It was agreed this would be monitored and reviewed.

(continued)

The LSU manager had given input in several staff meetings and was also now teaching some lessons of Maths on the main timetable, which had raised his profile with both staff and pupils. Staff as a whole reported more understanding of the referral process and the work within the LSU. Further work was agreed around the re-integration of pupils who had received support, and how this would be managed by staff receiving pupils back into lessons.

Further issues identified for action by the staff

- A complete revision of the timetable to reduce movement between the two buildings
- Implementation of a system of merit slips that could be exchanged for vouchers
- Review of the re-integration of pupils from the LSU to manage the transition after intervention

Communication and negotiation is an essential part of each stage of the cycle. If all staff are fully involved in the process they are more likely to support changes in the system.

Evaluating

Evaluation of the changes made is vital. This needs to be done with the gathering of follow-up information. Conclusions as to the effectiveness of changes or interventions can then be based on evidence.

This evaluation can become the first part of the next cycle.

Evidence-based system change: case study, part four

Evaluating changes made as a result of the initial audit

Data gathered about the changes made to the timetable to reduce movement between the two teaching blocks indicated that this was working well and there were fewer incidents reported here. It was decided to monitor this situation further and see if the improvements continued.

The rewards system continued to be an area of debate amongst staff, and further work was needed here.

The LSU manager, the learning mentor and the Special Educational Needs Co-ordinator had set up a referral panel supported by the Deputy Head, and this seemed to be working well both at allocating pupils' appropriate support, and also in feeding back to staff the outcome of referrals and planning for re-integration from the LSU.

The next stage of the audit process was a plan to consult with pupils and parents about the systems for rewards and sanctions.

This is the final stage of the review and planning cycle. The referral panel is another forum for continuing negotiation and communication. The evaluation can lead to another review and planning cycle with further changes for implementation.

Conclusion

School systems

- Changes in school systems can be very effective in helping to improve pupil behaviour.

- Planned change can empower all members of the school community to feel involved and committed to the change.

- Review of existing systems is vital if new initiatives are to work.

- Monitoring and evaluation are part of a cyclical process that leads to the next set of objectives in a gradual step-by-step process.

Suggestions for taking ideas forward

Audit

Consider the use of existing audit tools or whether you need to devise a new tool or adapt existing tools specifically for the purposes of your audit. For example, a general audit (like the one used in the case study example) may be a good starting point. When you want to conduct the next stage and, for example, consult with parents, using or adapting ideas from a different audit tool (e.g. the *Index for Inclusion* (CSIE 2000) or the *KS3 Behaviour and Attendance Review* (DfES 2003, in-depth sections)) may be helpful. It is unlikely that an existing audit tool will answer all your questions however, as every situation is unique.

To help you find the right tool you need to consider the broad questions you need answered. You also need to decide who is essential to include in the process, who it would be beneficial to include, and who else's views would be helpful. This may help with breaking the task down into manageable proportions.

Your plan will need to take into account available time and resources, but it is also worth remembering that careful planning will save much time, frustration and wasted effort in the long run. Learning Support Units that are planned effectively after reviewing existing systems, have had fewer problems establishing robust systems for proposing and supporting change.

Audits are time consuming and, if you want to gather potentially controversial information, can be difficult to conduct from the 'inside'. If you can enlist the help of your LEA Behaviour Support Team or another appropriate professional, this can give the process a more objective dimension. For example, deciding who from the school might be best placed to conduct interviews can be problematic. Will staff offer their real opinions if the senior management team are conducting the process? Or if support staff are conducting the process? Anonymous interviews (coded, as suggested in the case study) conducted by someone from outside the system may offer opportunities for staff to be more open about expressing their views.

Implementing change

After gathering people's views it is important to give them some feedback. We often forget to acknowledge how important contributors are to the process. Also, if analysis of data is fed back, it can be clarified that changes being made are based on contributions and suggestions, and not just randomly decided.

Different groups may require feedback in different ways:

- Teachers via staff meetings or training days
- Pupils via tutor time or PHSE where relevant
- Parents via letter or news bulletins.

It is also important to inform participants, either through the suggested forums or separately, about changes to be made to the system and how these changes are being monitored. Reviewing and changing a system needs to be a cyclical process, where changes are monitored and further changes made if necessary to continue to improve the system. Every monitoring and evaluation stage becomes a new mini review.

The role of the LSU manager

- *What are the many facets of the LSU manager's role?*

- *How can the LSU manager's role be developed and enhanced?*

What is the role of the LSU manager?

The role of the LSU manager, how it is defined and communicated within the school, is vitally important. The role has various functions, including:

1 Promoting the LSU as a whole school initiative

2 Assessing pupils' needs and planning an appropriate programme of intervention

3 Communicating with other staff about pupils and their needs

4 Influencing the practice of other staff, including providing training and support to other staff

5 Linking to the PSP process

6 Developing and maintaining links with families and other agencies

It is worth taking each of these elements and looking at them in more detail.

Promoting the LSU as a whole school initiative

The LSU manager and the senior management team

The LSU needs to be seen as part of a whole school initiative to tackle disaffection and challenging behaviour; in this way it will have more impact. If the LSU is conceptualised as a whole school resource it will be part of the continuum for pupils with challenging behaviours. Part of this conceptualisation is the philosophy of the senior management team, and therefore the dissemination of a whole school ethos which includes reflecting on the provision of teaching and learning for the whole school community. Riley and Rustique-Forrester suggest priority actions for creating an inclusive teaching and learning environment, one of which is to:

> Encourage teachers to consider the role of pedagogy in managing behaviour, and to use a range of teaching and learning strategies to respond to the diversity of pupils' abilities and needs.
> (Riley and Rustique-Forrester 2002: 74)

The LSU manager needs to work in partnership with the senior management team in promoting positive behaviour management and reflective practice in supporting both staff and pupils within the school community. In many schools the direct line manager of the LSU manager is the Deputy Head. This direct link to senior management is very helpful in keeping the LSU at the forefront of the agenda in terms of whole school behaviour policy. The use of a steering group model, as discussed in Appendix 5, is another effective way of promoting the LSU as a whole school strategy, because core groups of staff are represented and can be part of developing the work of the LSU.

The LSU manager and the governors

When considering the LSU as a whole school initiative to give pupils support in developing their emotional, social and learning skills, the school governors have an important role to play. Governors have a role in monitoring and analysing *school* behaviour, rather than in the specifics of the day-to-day rewards offered in school (Barrow 2002). Their views should be sought on new initiatives and in reviewing how the school is developing its inclusive practice and the implementation of strategies at a whole school level. In the new *Key Stage 3 Behaviour and Attendance Review* (DfES 2003), the governors are a key part of the information-gathering strategy. Gaining the support of governors for the LSU can help with the promotion of the strategy as a whole school initiative. Many LSU managers have a regular slot with governors to provide feedback on progress and issues for consideration.

Pupils who may access the LSU and promoting a whole school initiative

Within the framework of an initiative for promoting the provision of effective teaching and learning for the whole school community, it is worth reflecting on the pupils who may access the LSU. Pupils exhibiting challenging behaviour present an obvious target group, but care needs to be given when placing pupils within groups so that the dynamics of the group can promote a positive outcome.

There are other pupils who could benefit from the intervention offered in the LSU and some of these pupils are not causing problems but instead are disengaged from the school process.

> These students are not intentionally barred from the educational process; theirs is a passive form of exclusion, which is defined by the failure of the inclusion process. If we think of excluded students as having their invitation to learn withdrawn, we think of these 'invisible' students as never really having anything more than a half-hearted invitation in the first place.
>
> (Cooper *et al.* 2000: 10)

Other groups of pupils may access support in the LSU including pupils who have problems with attending school for various reasons, pupils who need extra support for a short period of time because of illness or bereavement within their families, and pupils having problems with specific areas of the curriculum.

The LSU 'space' can also be used for other purposes, including lunchtime clubs, a homework club, etc., which may encourage other pupils to access the space and minimise any stigma attached with using the 'room'.

Assessing pupils' needs and planning an appropriate programme of intervention

Prior to any intervention, baseline data needs to be collected and targets set with pupils and other staff as to the desired outcomes of the intervention. These targets need to be realistic and broken into small steps. Using this procedure can model a way of working for other staff. Academic baselines should be available through subject teachers, and the key areas are literacy and numeracy. An up-to-date reading and spelling test is useful information to clarify how a particular pupil is progressing. With this information the intervention programme and re-integration process can be planned. If, for example, a pupil has a low reading age and is struggling in science, and it is clear that the work set in science would be very difficult for this pupil to access, preparatory work can be undertaken with the science department before re-integrating the pupil into the lesson.

In addition, a behaviour baseline is needed. There are many behaviour checklists available and these need to considered in the school context. Such checklists include the Boxall Profile (Bennathan and Boxall 1998), Toward Better Behaviour (Jolly and McNamara 1992) and the Coping in Schools Scale (CISS) (McSherry 2001).

Some LSU managers feel reticent about asking overloaded staff for more information in the form of a behaviour checklist. However, this information is needed in order to plan appropriate intervention and support for pupils. The LSU staff cannot know how the pupil is coping in all his/her lessons and without this information planning withdrawal versus support sessions is very difficult. It is important that vital information about what the pupil 'is good at' is recorded too, to enable an opportunity to work in a positive way with the pupil. The other vital component of this 'partnership' with pupils is their assessment of themselves. In working with pupils I would always start from their assessments of themselves, even if these are not a reflection of the staff concerns (McSherry, 2001). It is important to assess pupils' needs appropriately – academically, socially and emotionally.

Communicating and negotiating with other staff about pupils and their needs

Keeping all staff informed about the work of the LSU generally and about the progress and needs of individual pupils is a good way of promoting positive strategies and areas of success that can be developed. To plan effectively for pupils receiving the support of the LSU, detailed information from the staff who teach those pupils is needed. Staff providing this information also need feedback about how this information has been used and any strategies that seem to have worked. When re-integrating pupils the active involvement of other staff makes the process easier and more effective (some examples of ways of involving staff in the re-integration process are explored in Chapter 4). There are various ways of keeping staff informed, depending upon the size of the school and the Key Stage of the pupils involved. For example, maintaining intensive and useful dialogue with a Key Stage 2 referring teacher may be easier to plan into a programme than it is for the range of teachers at Key Stage 3, but it is equally important to think through this process for all stages. Some ideas used in secondary schools have been:

- Including targets and successes in a weekly school bulletin

- Using a regular feedback slot at a staff meeting

- Attending Year team meetings on a rotational basis

- Attending curriculum team meetings on a regular basis

- Having a regular timetabled drop-in session where teaching and other staff can access the LSU staff for advice, support and updated information.

In primary schools planned time with class teachers of referred pupils seems to be a common model and can be part of the referral plan developed with staff.

Influence on the practice of other staff including providing training and support

If part of the LSU manager's role is to support and challenge other staff (and I think it should be) as well as pupils, then the role needs to be given status and support by the senior management team. The work of the LSU should be key in any whole school planning on behaviour management.

> The most effective forms of professional development are not always outside the school, but can occur through providing teachers with the time, resources, and opportunity within their own school to develop ways of monitoring the effects of changes on specific pupils, and to share experiences with colleagues and other professionals.
>
> (Riley and Rustique-Forrester 2002: 83)

The following case study example discusses some of the ways in which this can happen in an informal and planned way.

Case study: The Holly Hall School

The wider role of a Learning Support Unit manager

Context

The Holly Hall Secondary School is a mixed oversubscribed 11–16 urban, ethnically diverse school in Dudley, which serves a socially disadvantaged area. Forty per cent of pupils are from ethnic minority groups and 27 per cent have free school meal entitlement. In September 2002 we achieved Mathematics and Computing Specialist School Status. The Learning Support Unit, known as the Individual Learning Zone, opened at Easter 2002 with the principal aim of supporting pupils who were at serious risk of disaffection and/or exclusion. There are two members of staff who work within the Individual Learning Zone (ILZ): myself, the ILZ manager, and a full-time teaching assistant.

Role of the Learning Support Unit manager

Within the ILZ my principal responsibility is to co-ordinate the strategic direction, development and provision of inclusive education. My main duties are to:

- Play a key role in developing and implementing the school's inclusion policy
- Oversee the daily management of the school's ILZ
- Promote approaches that raise the quality and achievements of inclusive education for vulnerable pupils
- Liaise with and co-ordinate the contribution of external agencies
- Have a teaching commitment in the ILZ
- Contribute to the identification of effective inclusive teaching and learning approaches
- Maintain effective partnerships between parents and the school's staff promote pupils' learning, and provide information to parents about achievement and progress.

My role also involves the leading and managing of staff. My duties within this remit are to:

- Enhance the expertise of staff through demonstration and provide best practice to meet a diversity of pupils' inclusive educational needs

(*continued*)

■ Provide regular information to the Special Educational Needs team on the evaluation of the effectiveness of inclusive provision, to inform decision-making and policy review

■ Co-ordinate the work of the teaching assistant based in the ILZ.

The wider role of the LSU manager

Within the school I have additional roles which enhance my primary role as the ILZ manager. I am the Assistant Head of Year 7, which has enabled me to be involved in the primary–secondary transition and early identification of pupils who may require intervention through the ILZ after their move to the secondary school. It is envisaged that this role will be developed further, with me visiting pupils and working with them within their primary school. The main focus will be to work with pupils within years 5 and 6 who have been identified as possibly struggling with the transition to secondary school.

I have recently taken the role of Gifted and Talented Co-ordinator. The reasons behind this have been due to the developments with the ILZ. Although our primary focus is to work with pupils who are at serious risk of exclusion, we are finding that some of the pupils we work with are gifted and/or talented but disaffected. I therefore felt that the role would allow me to access support at an LEA level in order to develop support programmes and the curriculum for gifted and talented students within the ILZ and across the mainstream. We are currently in the process of developing a programme of Emotional Coaching for gifted and talented pupils, which will be facilitated through the ILZ.

In September 2003 my role as the ILZ manager is to develop further as I have been assessed as an Advanced Skills Teacher. This role is facilitating my work in the primary schools as mentioned earlier. Another part of this role is to develop the idea of intervention strategies and develop Emotional Literacy within the school and within our main primary feeder schools. I feel that becoming an Advanced Skills Teacher is an important and exciting development for those working in the area of additional education needs. We need to promote and develop further the work that is successfully implemented in LSUs, and the ability for Advanced Skills Teachers to have specific time for outreach work is a vehicle to share this good practice.

From September 2003 I shall have a fixed teaching timetable within the mainstream school. I shall be teaching mainly within Key Stage 3, primarily in the lower half of the year groups. Although this means that I shall be out of the ILZ far more than previously, I believe this is an important development as it enables me to work with departments on the key ideas and philosophies we follow within the ILZ. This, in turn, makes the integration of pupils from the ILZ back into the mainstream class more cohesive. It will also strengthen the relationship with some mainstream staff who perhaps do not fully understand the role of the LSU manager. It will enable them to see the successful transfer of skills from working in the ILZ with a select number of pupils to the mainstream class with a range of abilities.

Using the term 'training' to encompass the development of the skills of other staff, the examples used throughout this chapter illustrate ways in which the LSU manager can influence and develop the practice of colleagues in positive ways without organising training days or running workshops. Developing appropriate opportunities to communicate with colleagues about pupils and their needs, and the collaborative development of strategies that can be used to work with a range of pupils are all a part of continuing professional training and development.

Links to the Pastoral Support Programme (PSP) process

As part of the *Social Inclusion: Pupil Support* guidance (DfEE 1999a), schools were required to put in place strategies to prevent pupils being permanently excluded. This was in response to growing concerns about the long-term social implications of excluding pupils and to research reflecting the key groups of pupils it affected.

> Pupils who do not respond to school actions to combat disaffection may be a serious risk of permanent exclusion or criminal activity, and may need a longer term intervention to keep them from dropping out of school altogether. Teachers should actively identify such young people. Each one will need a Pastoral Support Programme worked up with external services.
>
> (DfEE 1999a: 27)

A PSP should be a positive meeting where all those involved with the pupil get together with that pupil (if possible) to put into place a supportive plan of action. Although the reasons why everyone is concerned must be expressed, the meeting is about finding a way forward. Therefore the underlying purpose is not to lay blame but to find alternative strategies for the pupil and school to try (McSherry 2001). In many schools the LSU managers have a clear link with the PSP process. Many pupils who may be placed on a PSP have accessed, or are accessing the support of the LSU. As part of a continuum of support the LSU is integral to the process of providing support at varying levels to pupils who are in danger of exclusion. This is not, as previously mentioned, the only role of the LSU; it may be that access to the LSU is inappropriate for a pupil on a PSP, or is only part of the package of support a pupil is receiving.

Developing and maintaining links with families and other agencies

Part of the LSU manager's role for pupils who are accessing support is to develop links with other agencies, e.g. Child and Adolescent Mental Health Services (CAMHS), Social Services and the LEA Behaviour Support Team. In LSUs where these links are well developed and maintained by the manager, it is undoubtedly the case that pupils receive support more efficiently and also that the manager has access to professional advice and support where this is needed.

A well-established link with the parents and carers of pupils accessing the LSU is also essential. Although this is often difficult to initiate, it pays huge dividends to the work that can be undertaken with the pupil in school when the parents/carers are 'on side'. LSUs use a variety of strategies to try and develop these relationships, including:

Action with parents

- Initial visits to the LSU before the intervention starts
- Planning with parents/carers for the outcome of the intervention
- Weekly phone calls home with good news
- Home–school diaries
- Parenting groups, either drop-in groups on specified days or a specific parenting course
- Home visits

Action for parents

- Working with the school's Learning Mentor, where there is one, to develop any of the preceding ideas
- Giving parents information about local support groups and agencies

The following case study example illustrates some effective work with the family of the referred pupil, as well as the pupil himself. The school involved wished the case study to remain unattributed.

Case study on family work

Adrian's Year 8 attendance record showed a pattern of frequent Monday 'illnesses' authorised by his mother. By half term, he was often away on Tuesdays as well. After Christmas, Adrian had a full week off school with a cold. His mother told school she had taken him to the doctor, who said Adrian had a post-viral infection. He was off for another two weeks. His school friends said he was fine and 'faking it'. After half term he still did not return, and a phone call home ascertained that Adrian was now unwilling to come back to school at all. His mother said she did not know what to do with him. His Head of Year managed to persuade him to come back for a morning, but he had run off by break time. His mother blamed the school for not tackling bullying – she herself had felt bullied at school. Adrian's two older brothers, both unemployed and at home all day, had become disaffected and never completed school. His father, who lived at home, appeared to play no role. Adrian was saying nothing to anyone and going nowhere fast.

When the Head of Year referred the case to the Learning Support Centre (LSC), the family work began. The Head of the LSC visited the home with the Education Welfare Officer (EWO) and met with Adrian and his mother. The atmosphere was strained; there was a lot a lot of anger directed at school from Mrs M., and Adrian visually checked with his mother each time before he spoke. The EWO outlined the legal situation, explaining how things had changed since Adrian's brothers were at school. Then Adrian, Mrs M. and the LSC teacher agreed a plan for the remaining three days of the week, starting with what Adrian felt able to commit to – which was one hour, in school in the LSC, being collected and dropped back by LSC staff.

Collecting Adrian, it became clear that his difficulty was leaving home, rather than coming to school. However, support continued on a practical basis, and emotionally starting from what the family was willing to talk about. Over the next ten days, Adrian made good progress. Conversations with Mrs M. on the doorstep every day became more relaxed and a level of trust started to build up gradually. Casual contact with one of Adrian's brothers confirmed that he wished he had finished school, and he agreed to encourage Adrian to go to school rather than hang around watching TV with him. Days when Adrian hit a blip, Mrs M. actually rang the LSC to ask for help, rather than having to be rung by school. That was an important shift.

It was important that the family and his friends supported Adrian, rather than depending on school. Adrian found it hard getting the courage to walk to and from school, but the onus of the responsibility for getting him to school was gradually shifted from the LSC to home, starting one day at a time, and fixing up friends to walk with him, days when his mum or dad could bring him, and even, on two occasions, the financial commitment of the family paying for a taxi.

Once Adrian was getting to school, the doorstep conversations were replaced by regular phone calls, reporting back good news as often as possible. Adrian was also allowed to ring and check in with home, from school, if he wanted to. After the next holiday break, the LSC wrote summarising Adrian's achievements, and asking Mr and Mrs M. into school to discuss the next half term's plan. Only Mrs M. turned up. This in itself was an achievement, as she confessed she had not been inside the school since she herself left

(continued)

prematurely. This meeting gave an opportunity to bring up the worries Adrian had shared about home, including some worries about domestic violence towards his mother from one of his brothers, and the threat of divorce. Adrian felt that he was the one who needed to stay at home to stick up for his mother.

The next week, Mr and Mrs M. came to school for a further meeting. Adrian joined the meeting half way through. Although it was not the LSC's role to try to heal the rift between Adrian's parents, the unit was able to help them see the effect it was having on Adrian and his education. The LSC was also able to put them in touch with a substance abuse agency to help address the problems fuelling their other son's violence.

Later that term, both parents were phoned and reminded about the Year 8 evening – and both attended. Staff (forewarned) were welcoming and positive about Adrian's achievements. Mrs M. had tears in her eyes when she left, saying she wished she had done it before.

At the end of term, Adrian's dad came to the LSC Parents' Morning to see Adrian receive his certificate congratulating him on improved attendance, and a photo of him wall climbing – a visual reminder of him achieving something he never thought possible. The Parents' Morning is a formal way of closing a case and saying to the family that targets have been met and that the student is now ready and able to succeed in mainstream school without direct LSC support.

I don't think anyone believes that Adrian's school life will be all plain-sailing until the end of Year 11, but the relationship established with Adrian, his parents and his brothers means that it should be easier to address the next difficulty.

This case study illustrates an LSU manager linking with a number of other agencies to provide appropriate support for a pupil and his family. Communication with other staff about the strategies used, and the success of the family links in promoting a positive outcome for this pupil, will not only aid his re-integration into the school community but could be a way of developing and influencing the good practice of other staff within the school.

Conclusion

- The LSU manager's role is multi-faceted and needs the full support of the senior management team to develop it to its full potential.

- The LSU manager needs to assess pupils adequately prior to the intervention in order to offer the best support to both staff and pupil.

- Communicating and negotiating with staff about pupils is essential and needs to be planned; it is a key part of the role.

- Helping other staff develop their expertise in working with challenging pupils is also a key part of the LSU manager's role.

- The LSU manager is likely to be a key player in the PSP process if it is seen as part of a whole school continuum of support for pupils presenting challenging behaviours.

- Communicating with parents/carers and outside agencies is vital to offer a holistic approach to a pupil's needs, and the manager needs adequate time to develop and maintain these links.

Suggestions for taking ideas forward

> While schools and teachers cannot alone overcome all the social, emotional and behavioural difficulties that most students will, at some time, experience, the conditions for learning that students encounter in school will always play a crucial role in promoting (or inhibiting) their active and positive engagement in the social and academic life of the community.
>
> (Cooper *et al.* 2000: 10)

How will you as an LSU manager communicate and negotiate with colleagues to promote the idea that the context of the school is a vital component in the plan made for individual pupils?

Are there ways in which you can develop your role to enhance your work with parents, to include them in the positive aspects of the school's role with their child?

How can communication with other staff be enhanced to develop effective practice in working with pupils with challenging behaviour?

What specific small steps can the school as a whole take to try and promote disenfranchised pupils' 'active and positive engagement' in school life?

Entry and exit criteria and strategies for promoting effective re-integration

- *How are clear entry criteria developed?*

- *How are effective referral procedures developed (including the use of in-school referral panels)?*

- *How are pupils involved in the process?*

- *How are exit criteria clarified?*

- *How is successful re-integration ensured?*

Developing clear entry criteria

For the LSU to be effective there needs to be clear entry criteria and referral procedures. These criteria can include a number of factors depending on the school and the model of LSU being used. The criteria and the procedures both need to be presented in a series of statements to ensure consistency. The criteria and procedures for referral need to be adhered to: if you accept casual referrals in the corridor from a frantic member of staff once it will not be long before you have an internal exclusion room and little idea of what it is you are meant to be achieving.

Who are the pupils that your provision can support? In the past excluded and high profile pupils more readily presented themselves, but what about the 'invisible' pupils who are passively excluded and are excluding themselves by being disengaged? Widening the scope of the work of the LSU to include the latter group also opens up dialogue within the school community about inclusion and behavioural needs. All pupils are entitled to a positive learning environment, and the LSU can be part of a wider whole school initiative to positively address the pupils' needs. Pupils who exhibit challenging behaviour may be stopping other pupils from receiving their entitlement. This is a hard argument to ignore when clearly on one level at least it is true. However, the other side of this argument is that the pupils disrupting classes are not being provided with an appropriate and engaging curriculum.

Conceptualising the LSU as part of a whole school approach to working with pupils is vital. All staff need to understand from the outset that this provision is part of a wider strategy, not an answer or an end point for a small group of disruptive pupils.

Different types of entry criteria

Using exclusion data

Targeting groups of pupils who may benefit from access to the LSU is part of the initial thinking process. Using data that the school collects about exclusions can be one way

Table 4.1 Sample exclusion data

Group	Number of fixed term exclusions this group has received	Number of pupils in group	Number of pupils in this group subsequently excluded permanently	Percentage of original group who ended up permanently excluded (%)
A	2	14	2	14
B	3	5	2	40
C	4	3	2	67

forward. Many schools collect data but do not use it in the planning of intervention strategies. For example, in analysing fixed term exclusion data, patterns may emerge that give a clear indication of the most effective timing of interventions. A clear pattern emerges from the data in Table 4.1.

The data does not hold any great suprises, in that we might have anticipated that pupils receiving larger numbers of fixed term exclusions were more likely to end up permanently excluded. However, the fact that a much lower percentage of those pupils with two fixed term exclusions ended up permanently excluded than those receiving higher numbers of exclusions gives us an indication of the preferred timing of an intervention. If we work with group A and prevent them from moving into group B or C, this will be a proactive move. It also means we are working with a group that have a higher chance of remaining in school if we can prevent them receiving any more fixed term exclusions. Work with pupils in group C has less chance of success and needs to be planned differently.

Using this data it might be decided that pupils who have received two fixed term exclusions need to be referred for additional support and considered at the referral panel (which is discussed in a later section in this chapter). The use of such criteria for referral may depend on how liberally the school uses fixed term exclusions as a way of controlling challenging behaviours. In some schools LSU staff are involved in 'return from exclusion' meetings, and all pupils returning from an exclusion of more than two days spend some time in the LSU (two or three days) and are then gradually re-integrated into all classes over a week. This approach offers the opportunity to work with the young person – to consider the reasons for exclusion and ways to avoid this in the future – in a positive way. It also allows LSU staff to work with the pupil to repair damaged relationships with other staff and pupils before returning to classes. This sort of approach can only work in a school where there are relatively few exclusions and more than one member of staff working in the LSU, which allows for more flexible approaches.

Targeting particular year groups or Key Stages
In many schools the LSU provision is targeted at particular Key Stages or year groups. For example, many primary Learning Support Units target pupils in years 5 and 6 and many secondary LSUs initially targeted Key Stage 3. Targeting an age group of pupils does make referrals more manageable. For primary pupils, targeting years 5 and 6 means that the vulnerable and 'at risk' pupils are offered additional support in the build-up to the transition to secondary school.

In some areas the secondary schools target year 7 (within the first term), offering additional support at the other side of the secondary transfer for this 'at risk' group. In a previous publication (McSherry 2001) an early intervention programme aimed at pupils who were vulnerable at the primary–secondary transfer was outlined. Part of the programme aimed to work with secondary schools to put in place support for pupils as soon as they transferred, minimising difficulties for many pupils. A further development is the increased use of learning mentor and LSU support for these pupils as soon as they arrive at secondary schools. The initial reasons for highlighting support for Key Stage 3 was a reflection of the limited range of options otherwise available for younger secondary age pupils. In Key Stage 4 many schools adopt a more flexible approach for pupils who are finding the mainstream curriculum inaccessible.

Using the LSU as a re-integration base for non-attenders or school refusers

Some secondary LSUs are offering support for pupils returning to school after a long absence. This support tends to be only one of a raft of interventions offered by these LSUs and not the only type of programme available. Careful consideration does need to be given to the balance of needs of pupils within the LSU – a group of very challenging year 10s may not be the most ideal mix for a group of Key Stage 3 school refusers.

The entry criteria for each LSU may vary depending upon the needs of the school (or group of schools) within which the LSU is based. Entry criteria need to be made explicit and presented within a positive preventative framework. There also needs to be clarity within the whole school pastoral system about what interventions and strategies should already have been used before a referral to the LSU is considered; for example, referrals and support within subject departments from tutors, and preliminary work with parents to try and understand the reasons why a pupil is not thriving within the school. At a primary level the school SENCo and senior management team may have been involved in supporting both the staff member and pupil who is experiencing difficulties and in working closely with the parents.

Leaflets for parents, pupils and staff should explain these criteria. The entry criteria and preventative framework are part of and need to be included in the aims of the LSU. Review of the entry criteria should be undertaken through the steering group (discussed in Appendix 5) to reflect the changing needs of the school, or group of schools. Review of the entry criteria may also need to be undertaken if the evaluation of the interventions indicate that they are not as successful as anticipated.

A common mistake in new LSUs is to work initially with the most difficult pupils, those on the verge of permanent exclusion (those indicated in Table 4.1 as having a small chance of remaining within the school). This first cohort consequently is often unsuccessful, leaving the manager feeling a failure and all the 'doubters' within the school feeling vindicated in their belief that nothing can work. This was an inappropriate group of pupils for the intervention planned. Using the LSU as an earlier stage in the continuum of provision is likely to be more effective.

Even if there is clarity about the entry criteria to the LSU (what work the unit aims to do and which pupils might fit these criteria), there is still a need for a robust referral procedure. This procedure will gather information, filter referrals and balance the groups of pupils accessing the provision at any one time. A robust referral procedure should also prompt school staff to consider the full range of strategies available at each level of the continuum. There should only be considered referrals to the LSU. Having an established procedure ensures that the LSU is not used as an instant internal exclusion room for pupils excluded from their classes.

The size of the LSU and the number of staff allocated to the provision will affect the diversity of approaches possible. The timetabling of the LSU provision, and the amount of time allocated to each group of pupils, will also affect the entry criteria for the specific LSU. For example, if the LSU offers three groups of pupils sessions each day of the week there may be a limited amount of time to offer systematic support for pupils returning from exclusions.

Some examples of entry criteria are:

■ Disruptive challenging behaviour

■ Internal truancy (i.e. from subject lessons)

■ External truancy (i.e. non-attendance at school)

■ Withdrawn or anti-social behaviour

■ School phobia

■ Students at risk of exclusion

■ Key Stage 3 pupils unable to cope with a full school day

■ Long-term absentees for gradual re-integration

■ Pupils re-integrating from the Pupil Referral Unit (PRU).

Referral procedures

Referral to the LSU needs to be part of a whole school systematic approach to behaviour management. School systems should reflect a staged approach to dealing with problems and all staff need to be clear about the referral procedures and criteria. It is important that pupils are able to continue to attend those lessons in which they are successful throughout any intervention from the LSU. This is not only considered to be good practice (Ofsted 2003) but is essential for effective re-integration. It offers us the opportunity to work with the pupils to build on their strengths. It is also vital to seek the pupils' views and work with them in building on their strengths.

An example of the importance of asking pupils' views can be illustrated through one school where there seemed to be a particular problem with pupils not wanting to attend the LSU. In fact, for some, their behaviour deteriorated during the intervention. On exploring the issue with pupils it transpired that many had been taken out of lessons they liked and felt that they had been good at. They reported that they felt angry and confused because they thought they were being rejected by teachers they had felt successful with. Clearly this had not been the aim of the intervention, but detailed baseline data and clear planning for individual pupils had not taken place. Involving pupils in the referral is part of the process of developing their ownership and motivation for involvement in the programme on offer. Pupils assessing themselves and setting targets based on their perceptions of the problems are fundamental parts of the process (McSherry 2001).

An example of a referral procedure in a secondary school might include:

Stage 1   Pupil disrupts a particular lesson several times and is referred to the Head of Department. The tutor is also informed. The parents are informed.

Stage 2   After input from the Head of Department further disruption is referred to to the Head of Year. The tutor is also informed. The parents are informed.

Stage 3   Head of Year meets with parents to develop an action plan.

Stage 4   Pupil is a cause for concern across more than one subject area and/or in unstructured times, and the case is referred to the referral panel for allocation of additional in-school support. Information and data is collected for the referral panel to inform discussion and decisions as to the most appropriate support.

This procedure is illustrated in Figure 4.1.

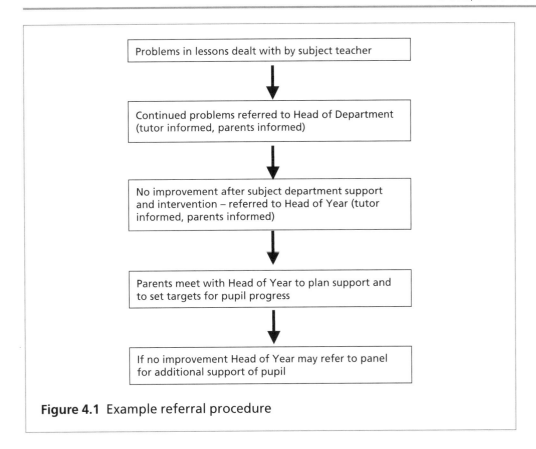

Figure 4.1 Example referral procedure

A primary referral procedure might look different but would also include evidence of the problem being more than a personality clash or specific to one particular situation. There would be indications that other strategies had been tried and that the problems were persisting over time and in a variety of situations.

Referral forms

A key element in establishing a procedure is an effective and informative referral process. Referral forms need to include a range of information, including strategies already tried and how these have worked. The information you ask for on a referral form will be influenced by the aims of the intervention. You may ask very basic questions in the first instance, as illustrated in the case study on page 33, or gather more information even at this first stage, as illustrated in the example format in Appendix 2. This is an example only and any form needs to meet the needs of your setting and context.

This form would constitute the first part of a process and, hopefully, provide enough information for a referral panel to make some judgement about the most appropriate support approach. Once this decision had been made additional information would be needed, depending on the intensity of the support/intervention required. I would suggest that if the pupil is going to spend time in the LSU you will need more in-depth and extensive information in order to plan an appropriate intervention.

The collection of information before an intervention allows you to develop an informed and evidence-based programme for the pupils, with a clear idea of outcomes and therefore exit strategies. You will need a range of baseline data, and therefore some assessment may need to take place. Some of this information will already be collated in the school, for example literacy and numeracy levels, reading age, etc. Some may not be collected on a regular basis, for example an assessment of current behaviour. It is also important that pupils make assessments of themselves.

Communication with staff about the use of the information you have collected is an important next stage. As you are going to use this information to plan your work with the pupils it is good practice to share this with the staff who provided the information in the first place. It is impossible to plan your work effectively without their input, and feeding this back is a way of keeping them 'on side'. It is also important to continue strong links between the pupils and their tutors and Head of Year.

Referral panels

Referral panels are one strategy used by schools to streamline the use of additional support and to cut down on paperwork. These panels can take referrals for all pupils needing extra support. They typically meet on a regular basis to discuss pupils and match resources to need, and include representatives from all the staff groups offering support. Ideally they include a senior manager as this gives status to the process and also allows decisions to be made within the group and without having to be referred on for further consideration by the SMT.

Referral panel membership in a secondary school – an example

Deputy Head

SENCo

Literacy Co-ordinator

Head of EMA (Ethnic Minority Achievement)

Inclusion Co-ordinator (also LSU manager)

Lead Learning Mentor

Connexions Personal Adviser

The above is an example of the panel membership in one secondary school; other schools also include representative Heads of Year or Heads of Key Stages. The model used will reflect the structure of the pastoral system within the school.

In a primary school the panel model is equally useful and, as most primary LSUs are linked units, panels will include representatives from linked schools. As in the secondary school example, the panel should reflect the range of support available in the school so that professionals can plan together for the most appropriate support for individual pupils.

Referral panel membership for a primary linked LSU – an example

Deputy Heads or key link personnel from both schools

SENCos from both schools

Additional support teachers (working in the schools) as appropriate; may include Ethnic Minority Achievement, literacy support, behaviour support, etc.

LSU manager

Learning Mentors (if applicable)

The benefits of this process are:

- One form for all referrals, which cuts down on staff frustration and paperwork overload.

- It allows for planned professional input for pupils with a range of problems and allows support staff to feel empowered to make informed decisions about their work.

- It provides opportunities for a discussion of cases with colleagues, which in turn allows for informed longer-term planning for individual pupils and groups of pupils.

- It ensures that referrals and the planning of support is part of a whole school approach.

- It removes the duplication of support that can occur, especially in a large secondary school.

- It is possible to plan input from other agencies into a session where all support staff can be part of discussions, and the value of different perspectives.

Possible problems

The timetabling of several members of staff to be free at one time can present problems and it is not always desirable for these meetings to be after school. Schools that hold these meetings either in school time or as part of the regular meeting cycle find it works most effectively. Part of the decision is about giving the process high status as an effective method of providing a whole school approach to managing support.

Sometimes it can take a running-in period before all staff get used to the new system, especially if they have been used to referring pupils in the corridor, either verbally or by pupil name on a scrap of paper! However, feedback from schools who have implemented this system indicate that the advantages far outweigh the problems. The case study presented below illustrates one school's application of this type of panel.

Case study: Chestnut Grove School

Arriving at my school five years ago I was given the task of line-managing the Special Needs Department. This developed into the line management of the Learning Support Centre, the Learning Mentors and the Ethnic Minority Achievement team. For two years I 'managed' these teams, desperately trying to ensure that our students' various needs were met; however, frequently I felt as though the support structure could and should be improved.

Step one was to integrate these separate entities and place them under the umbrella of the 'Student Support Service'. The theory behind this was that each 'department' would remain independent but linked through the Student Support Service Panel. The underlying aims of the Panel were to ensure that support was spread equally around school to meet the needs of staff and students; moreover the Panel's aim was to get away from random moaning from staff asking and demanding 'What's happening for this child?'

Step two was to get the other members of the Senior Management Team to recognise the value and importance of a group of staff meeting in school time. This would mean that staff could not be used for cover during this time, and that all members of the Panel had to attend the meetings.

Our final step was to try and work out how we could create an effective dialogue between the staff and the Panel. We wanted to get away from individuals moaning and from the idea that if you made a referral to the Panel then the child was no longer your responsibility – that they somehow disappeared into the ether of 'support'. This final step was undoubtedly our hardest and we made many mistakes.

(continued)

Our first mistake was the initial design of our referral form. We designed what we felt would be a simple form for members of staff to fill out, asking questions about grades, attendance – basic school information. Of course we had overlooked that many people making a referral to the Student Support Service were doing so because they felt in need of support, not because they wanted to trawl through files or walk down to the general office to copy from one form onto another information that would make our lives easier.

Various redesigns ensued. However, we could not get away from the fact that some staff felt that filling in a form meant that they were no longer responsible for meeting the needs of that student in their classroom. To all of us in the Student Support Service this was the key to creating a fully inclusive school. Finally we got rid of questions that asked for data on students and reduced the form to just three questions:

1 What type of referral are you making?

2 Explain briefly what hopes and expectations you might have from this referral.

3 What made you decide to make this referral now?

It's not perfect! But this simple step of changing the form has made a difference; and we keep on trying – this year we have reorganised Panel meetings, extending the membership and meeting fortnightly not weekly. And finally (after five years!) I am no longer dealing with requests on the corridor, staff complain less and support is more equally spread around departments and students.

A referral panel or similar systematic way of considering all referrals/requests for additional support for pupils enables support staff to consider the scope of the intervention they can offer and the appropriateness for each individual pupil. It saves school staff completing numerous different forms (or failing to do so because there are so many).

Exit criteria

Exit criteria often become a consideration for established LSUs as they review their systems, or at the end of a period of intervention. Yet having clear exit criteria is as important as the entry criteria. In order to be clear about the exit criteria we need to have a precise idea about what we aim to achieve. There are therefore some key questions to answer:

1 What is the aim of this intervention for this pupil or group of pupils?

2 How long will the intervention continue before it is reviewed to see what progress is being made towards the stated aims?

3 Which other staff members will be involved in reviewing progress?

4 How will staff involved with this pupil or group of pupils be worked with to ensure the most effective re-integration after the intervention?

The exit criteria need to be agreed prior to the intervention. The agreement will be easier if there is a clear referral system, a baseline to work from and a clear set of objectives for the intervention. For example, if the objective of the intervention is to reduce problems in certain lessons a key aim will be to re-integrate the pupil into those lessons. A time limit will need to be agreed for the programme and for the re-integration process. If re-integration is unsuccessful a new intervention will need to be planned, again with a clear set of objectives and a time limit otherwise pupils are in danger of just being removed indefinitely from a particular subject, and the LSU is in danger of being a dumping ground for pupils and not a part of a whole school approach. It is not always easy to keep track of the proportion of time pupils are out of their mainstream lessons, especially if they are accessing more than one strand of support. One way of trying to keep an overview of pupil support, and also to structure that support constructively, is via the use of a referral panel model, discussed in detail earlier in this chapter.

Decisions about pupils' support need to be based on both process (type of support, amount of support) and performance (progress with target behaviours, lessons, etc.) criteria. Pupils' views are also an important element of this process, and eliciting these views through interviews or questionnaires is one way of building a picture of types of input and their success. Pupil progress can be surveyed across the school as a way of assessing general patterns of behaviour. Classroom observations and re-application of baseline assessments are also ways of measuring progress and readiness to move on.

Pupils, parents and other staff need to be clear about the objective and the time limit of the intervention. If staff are aware that this pupil is returning, when they will be returning and what support is planned for both pupil and teacher, the re-integration itself is likely to be more successful than when a member of staff is shocked and angry because they thought this problem had gone away for ever!! When the intended outcomes of the work are set before the intervention starts, it enables effective evaluation to take place. Evaluation will be explored further in Chapter 6.

To ensure clear exit criteria you need to have clear baseline information and a clear set of objectives, and the intervention needs to be time limited. If, at the end of the planned intervention, further support is needed, the case can be taken back to the referral panel and a new support package planned. Decisions about pupils' support need to be based on both process and performance. Pupils' views and progress should be central to all planning.

Some examples of exit criteria are:

- Two terms of LSU support should be the maximum for most pupils.

- Student progress sheets collected from all subject teachers will indicate a general pattern of improvement in key behaviours.

- Observational data made by LSU staff of pupils in class indicate some improvement.

- Pupil's questionnaire indicates pupil's perception of changes (where appropriate) in behaviour in class, motivation, attitude and attendance.

- Improvement in pupil's pattern of internal exclusions, external exclusions and detentions.

Re-integration

Re-integration is one of the vital tests of successful LSU interventions. If pupils are not going to re-integrate back into mainstream classes, referral to an appropriate outside agency may be part of the LSU's role. However, if this is a consistent outcome of intervention you may need to re-clarify the referrals being made to the LSU, as a key role – re-integration – is not being fulfilled.

Pupils, parents and other staff need to be clear about the format of re-integration. They all need to be clear from the outset that re-integration is the final stage of the process – remaining in the LSU for the rest of the pupil's school career is not an option! The pupil's views about his/her readiness to re-integrate need to be taken into account, and some pupils will need more support with this process than others.

For effective re-integration we need a clear process for our work with pupils; we need clear entry criteria, clear baseline data, a programme planned on this information with clear targets and outcomes and clear exit criteria to re-integrate pupils into lessons as quickly as possible. It is also vital that throughout the intervention pupils continue to attend those mainstream lessons where they are successful. The re-integration itself is the end stage of a process of working ideally with staff, pupils and parents to effect change in the interactions that were causing problems. As was mentioned in Chapter 3, the LSU manager's role, if it is to effect long-term change in the school system itself, needs to be broader than working just with the pupils.

In the next two sections I will consider two approaches used by Learning Support Unit staff to ensure that other staff are engaged in the process of re-integration. Both approaches will be illustrated with case studies to give some detail about how the approaches have been used in practice. The first looks at an approach where the teacher and LSU manager 'swop roles' in relation to the pupil, to re-establish a relationship between a pupil and a teacher that has broken down. The second explores the use of solution focused meetings to prepare staff for a pupil's re-integration.

The school featured in the first two case study examples is a secondary school. It is not in an Excellence in Cities area. The LSU was initially funded through an LEA initiative, but the funding ends in March 2004. This LSU works as preventatively as possible, working with a relatively large number of pupils with lower levels of problems (i.e. these pupils are not about to be permanently excluded). Most pupils remain in their mainstream lessons for 90 per cent of the school week. There is a focus on working with families and including parents in frequent communications and feedback. This LSU also works with a number of different agencies to provide additional support to pupils, and works with mainstream staff to extend the skills of staff and develop more positive relationships between individual staff and pupils referred to the unit. The examples below illustrate this approach to working with other staff in the school to facilitate re-integration.

The school wished the case studies to be unattributed.

Case study on re-integration (example one)

Michael, a traveller boy, was in Year 7. He had been successfully integrated into 90 per cent of mainstream lessons after half a term of intensive support from the LSU. Lessons that were set, such as Maths, English and Science, were going fairly well. He was also doing well in practical lessons, where he was able to move round the classroom. Mixed ability, whole class subjects, however, were proving much more challenging for Michael and the teacher alike. In groups of 30 plus, despite best efforts at appropriate differentiation and in-class support, Michael was starting to act the class clown, and previously successful lessons were deteriorating rapidly for all concerned. The inevitable day came when the history teacher asked that Michael should be withdrawn from her twice-weekly lessons.

Conscious that removing Michael would create more problems than it would solve (including the obvious one of having to get him back in), it was suggested that the history teacher might like to teach Michael herself, either individually or in a small group, in the LSU, whilst the teacher in charge of the LSU taught the whole class.

A structure was agreed. The mainstream history teacher prepared the lesson plan and resources for the next four lessons. The LSU teacher suggested further ways of making the differentiated work accessible for Michael. Lesson one was a great success. Michael was clearly not only thrilled by the attention of one-to-one tuition, but also felt safe enough to try really hard, achieving at a level the history teacher had not previously envisaged. The history teacher was also happy – happy to have a chance to start to build the sort of individual relationship with a child that LSU staff often take for granted, and to be developing a different professional expertise from that of the whole class teacher. Back in the classroom, the LSU teacher was busy revisiting all those whole class teaching skills and pleasures that took her into teaching in the first place, as well as establishing credibility both with students and with other staff as someone who could hack

(continued)

the 32 as well as the 1. Finally, the Year 7 class themselves benefited from learning from a different adult, in a different style.

The second lesson repeated the successful formula of the first. But the final two lessons were amended, in that a small group of students joined Michael and the history teacher, building a bridge between individual and whole class. This gave Michael a chance to practise learning and behaving in front of others; it gave the others a chance to benefit from some more intensive help; and it gave the teacher an opportunity to practise and enjoy small group teaching skills.

Week 3 and, back in the main class, the LSU teacher joined the history teacher for the first part of the fifth lesson. This enabled all the students, but especially Michael, to be aware that all the adults were working together and sharing positive feedback. Michael was clearly more comfortable, and the history teacher felt that she had 'banked' some good will and subject knowledge with him, which she could draw on when necessary to get him back on task.

Interestingly, in the staff room, the history teacher talked openly about the different sort of pressure and tiredness one gets from individual and small group teaching, as well as reporting back positively on the working ethos of the LSU, whilst the LSU teacher was able to join in the general camaraderie of surviving 7JN on a Friday Period 5. It was a small design that ended up with a lot of quite complex bridges being built.

The second example raises an interesting and sometimes overlooked issue – the LSU staff taking over the role of the pastoral staff and in fact becoming 'the surrogate pastoral system for the pupil' (Ofsted 2003), a situation to be avoided if any hope of successful re-integration is to remain. This case study illustrates an approach that clearly asserts the tutor's pastoral role with this pupil.

Case study on re-integration (example two)

Having it happen successfully once, the LSU started to try to expand this way of working. Another Year 7 student was being supported by the LSU, but this time for complex emotional needs resulting from damaging home circumstances. The LSU was a very safe place for him, and the staff there were familiar with his difficulties. Re-integration must work, however, as much as for pastoral needs as for learning and behaviour needs, and John's form tutor was beginning to feel left out of the equation, posing the problem of how John was to be re-integrated back into the mainstream pastoral system, even though his difficulties would not have been fully resolved.

The initial discussions concerned John, and the LSU teacher discussed with him whether he was comfortable with his home situation being shared with his form tutor. More than accustomed to every professional under the sun knowing more about him than he knew himself, he had no problem with this, although he also felt it was not likely to be of much help. The following week, the head of the LSU and the form tutor met with John during a non-contact period. This was followed by a weekly session in which the teacher-in-charge of the LSU took the form registration whilst the tutor met with John – initially on his own, then sometimes with a small group. The LSU teacher benefited from getting to know that form much better (and it had several characters who either had been, or were shortly to be, referred to the Unit). John felt more comfortable asking his tutor for help, and as part of the form in general. Between the form tutor and John, they set up an exit system to her (rather than the LSU) if he was feeling stressed, and she was the one who begged and borrowed ties from the school office when the money ran out, and called home about Parents evening, thus beginning to establish a fragile working relationship with the father. The tutor was so pleased with the opportunity to have some 'quality time' with small groups from her form, that when the LSU teacher time was withdrawn, an arrangement was made for a learning support assistant from the LSU to support once a week, staying with the form while the tutor met individuals and small groups in the adjacent subject office.

Solution focused brief therapy meeting

The case study example illustrating this approach raises some important points that demonstrate why re-integration is such a difficult process, particularly in large secondary schools. Communication with other staff prior to the re-integration is vital if there is to be a consistent approach used with pupils who are re-integrating after an intervention in the LSU. Changing staff perceptions and attitudes about individual pupils (and sometimes groups of pupils) is an important part of the work if it is to be successful. This can be seen as a 'reframing' process. Reframing involves looking at the same event or situation from a different viewpoint. This approach is explored by Cooper *et al.* (1994) and is, in essence, about attempting to achieve a match between various parties' views of the same situation.

As an example let us take an offer of additional in-class support offered to a pupil. The pupil may feel awkward about receiving additional in-class support, refuse to accept it and deal with the situation by becoming abusive to staff. The pupil may see the learning support as 'showing her up' in front of her peers. The teaching staff may have seen the same support in a very positive light, as additional help for the pupil. So their views of the same situation are very different, in fact so different that it has caused conflict. The way to break the cycle of negative behaviour is for both parties to change their response. From discussions it may be possible for the pupil to see the support in a more positive light, and also allow the teaching staff to offer the support in a way that does not embarrass the pupil. If we are aware that some pupils find it more difficult to engage because of the position they find themselves in, the challenge is to engage them despite this – not to reject them because of it.

One of the positive elements of involving other staff in an open and positive dialogue about pupils is that they can 'reframe' their perceptions about individual pupils, as Riley and Rustique-Forrester (2002) discovered:

> The staff of one low excluding school told us that knowing about a pupil's situation at home provided a context for understanding and interpreting the behaviour of a pupil and enabled them to be more responsive and sensitive. As one teacher commented, 'If I know that that child didn't spend the night at home, I am not going to get on his case for having a dirty uniform.'
> (Riley and Rustique-Forrester 2002: 78–9)

Having a context does not make the behaviour more acceptable, but it can help with distancing the behaviour from a personal affront and also in enabling teachers to feel that they can make justifiable allowances. For example, involving a staff group in problem-solving around a group of very challenging pupils, and providing a context for the behaviour of individual pupils, can be very beneficial in allowing everyone to frame their concerns and anxieties appropriately. Having this context for individual behaviour is one aspect of this type of approach that teachers, on evaluating the input, have found particularly useful.

A solution focused approach starts with the assumption that an emphasis on the past and on the details of the problem is not necessary for the development of a solution. The example of a solution focused approach to re-integration is an approach being tried by one particular school. The school used in this example is an all-girls secondary school. The Learning Support Unit is part of a cohesive support department that caters for the needs of the pupils within the school.

Case study: Solution focused brief therapy approach to re-integration meetings at Burntwood School

My role at Burntwood is to lead the Social Inclusion Team. The team consists of myself, three Learning Mentors and a Learning Skills Centre Manager. The Centre is used to accommodate pupils who for various reasons cannot manage school. These include pupils who have been very ill, those returning from exclusion, some who have dropped an option and some excluded from individual lessons. Pupils in the Centre can be either part or full time. The Centre is very much a short-term provision and our aim is for full re-integration back into mainstream classes.

In reviewing the work of the Centre with our Educational Psychologist an identified weakness was the re-integration of pupils back into class. The pupils were being well prepared for this whilst in the Centre, receiving extra support from their mentors, discussing the particular problems they are having in class and strategies to deal with them. They set targets and the programme for re-integration was discussed with them so that they felt involved. However it was felt that we were not preparing the staff at all. We were not sharing the expertise, which exists among staff, nor what we had learned about pupils from having them in the Learning Skills Centre.

In a big school like Burntwood, effective communication can be difficult and time consuming, and the Educational Psychologist suggested that a 'case conference' type of meeting might be a way around this. I remembered having meetings where all the staff were called together, usually to discuss a pupil who was causing concern, and these meetings were often very negative. The meetings were taken up with discussing the problem and everyone was able to off-load their anger, often with the result that the pupil's poor reputation was confirmed and the teachers were left feeling helpless. Our Educational Psychologist suggested we used the solution focused brief therapy approach.

What I liked about the solution focused meeting is that it is very structured and each part is timed. We wrote out the stages that the meeting was going to follow with a time allocation, which meant that everyone was clear about what was going to happen. One person was there to chair the meeting and another to minute it.

The pattern for the meeting was:

5 minutes describing the family background

This was limited to a very brief history, outlining the significant events and maintaining confidentiality.

5 minutes sharing what staff felt were the problems

Prior to the meeting all staff were circulated with a questionnaire, which they were asked to return before the meeting (see Appendix 3). This asked for information about

what behaviour was causing concern

times when the pupil had done better.

This indicated whether there were problems across all subjects or whether they were restricted to particular subjects. Additional benefits of the questionnaire are that staff are able to focus their thinking before the meeting – having a list of the concerns beforehand means that they can be summarised in a shorter time, and there can be input from everyone even if some staff cannot attend the meeting.

30 minutes considering solutions

In this part we were able to uncover exceptions and competencies. We also discussed strategies that have worked and used scaling techniques. This technique explores on a scale of 1 to 10 (where 1 is the worst

(continued)

things could possibly be and 10 is the best), where the pupil is now. Questions can also be explored, such as 'What would have to happen to move this pupil from 3 to 4?' and 'What is keeping the pupil at 3?' The process aims to uncover strengths and effective strategies, and to clarify expectations. This in turn assists with setting realistic targets and observable goals

Feedback from staff about the solution focused approach included the following comments:

- the meetings were very positive
- the background information had really helped staff to understand the pupil and her behaviour
- staff welcomed the opportunity to share what had worked, and everyone felt they were going away with strategies which would benefit the pupil
- it was helpful that staff would all be doing the same thing, that everyone had been given the opportunity to have their say and that staff had been able to agree strategies; therefore there should be no confusion for the pupil and much clearer expectations.

To summarise, the advantages of the solution focused therapy approach are that staff:

- work with the pupil and not with the problem
- focus on what the pupil is doing well
- look to the future and how they want things to be
- explore what things are already contributing to the future
- treat the pupils as the experts in all possible aspects of their lives and use the pupils' perceptions and views of the situation
- learn to recognise and build on the skills and resources they as teachers are already using to change the situation.

Solution focused meeting in action

Example one

One pupil identified for such a meeting was a pupil who:

- has extremely complex and unusual family problems
- suffers from depression
- has panic attacks and doesn't want to go to class for fear of this happening
- finds travelling to school very difficult, following an incident. She often arrives late, upset and anxious
- has found herself isolated from her friends as a result of her poor attendance
- is a very private and shy person who has a real anxiety about people asking her questions about why she hasn't been in class and about her family, and is very anxious about the work she has missed and catching up because she is in her first year of GCSEs.

The solutions identified were:

- register the pupil in the Learning Skills Centre (a place where she feels 'safe')
- a 'time out' card to be used if the pupil feels a panic attack coming on
- staff agreement not to question the pupil about her absence and to discourage other pupils from commenting
- staff to praise the pupil privately for attendance and work

(*continued*)

- friends identified who the pupil works well with
- pupil to be assured that she does not need to make up missed work
- allowances made for homework not done and deadlines extended
- short term – the pupil to be escorted to class by an adult or trusted friend
- staff to use opportunities for paired or small group work
- agreed adjustments to PE kit to be worn
- agreement for Dance to be spent in Learning Skills Centre.

Example two

Behaviour which gives cause for concern:

- refuses to follow the school rules, e.g. wears the incorrect uniform
- eats and drinks in class, shouts out rather than putting her hand up, arrives late to lessons
- refuses to follow the teacher's instructions and gets angry at being told what to do (however reasonable the instruction)
- cannot remain focused on a task whether it's easy or more challenging
- frequently leaves her seat during a lesson
- cannot talk sensibly or politely to adults (some teachers said it is the same with her peers, others reported that she doesn't stop talking to other girls)
- responds to any interaction with teachers in an extremely aggressive, confrontational manner
- cannot accept any advice, criticism or instruction without a fight!
- acts in such a way that the other students are frightened of her (discreet bullying)
- distracting the teacher when she's trying to teach whole class and / or individuals.

Staff agreed that this pupil is better when

- she is not confronted and the behaviour is ignored
- she is getting one to one attention
- she is praised
- humour is used rather than anger
- she is the centre of attention (so, for example, this pupil enjoys class discussions)
- teachers wait until they have her full attention
- there are clear expectations
- there is no interaction with the teacher at all
- she can begin work straight away without having to listen to instructions or sit quietly
- explanations are short and clear
- instructions lead her through the task step by step, so she does not have to use her initiative
- she hasn't had any 'grief' with any staff that day
- she is not sitting next to friends
- she has her equipment and books
- tasks are set which can be completed in one lesson.

Solutions

There was a great deal of discussion about conflict management.

(continued)

The following solutions were agreed. Staff would:

- give careful consideration to where the pupil sits and it would be away from friends
- avoid confrontation by saying firmly, 'I need you to . . .' and walk away
- be clear in their expectations. 'I am the teacher and I want you to . . .'
- use a flat, monotone voice, mirroring what they want from her
- control their own feelings and not get angry with her
- use humour wherever possible
- praise wherever possible
- get the class started on a task quickly and keep instructions to a minimum
- set tasks which can be completed in a lesson and not carried over.

For LSU managers interested in exploring this approach further there are some excellent books on using the solution focused approach in school settings, for example, Rhodes and Ajmal (1995) and Ajmal and Rees (2001).

Re-integration – some thoughts

There are some key practical areas to consider when ensuring the most effective re-integrations. To offer the highest chance of success:

- Re-integration needs to be planned
- Use of solution focused meetings is useful
- Support for pupils and receiving staff needs to be considered
- Everyone needs to be clear what will happen if there is a problem

Some key questions about individual re-integration

What is the programme this pupil is accessing?

Why has this programme been chosen?

How will the pupil be re-integrated?

When will this begin?

What will need to be done before it starts?

Who will support this re-integration?

Are teachers aware that the pupil is returning?

Are they prepared and supported?

What is their role in the exit strategies?

Is the pupil clear about the re-integration process and what support is available?

Is the pupil aware of what to do if things are going wrong?

Are the parents aware of the re-integration process?

Are they aware of ways they could support their child in this process?

A re-integration audit or checklist may help with the process of evaluating your own practice.

Some key points covered in this chapter

Entry criteria

■ Entry criteria need to be made explicit and presented within a positive preventative framework.

Referrals

School systems

■ Referral to the LSU needs to be part of a whole school systematic approach to behaviour management.

■ School systems should reflect a staged approach to dealing with problems and all staff need to be clear about the referral procedures and criteria.

Pupils

■ Pupils should be in involved in the referral, assessment and target-setting process.

■ Pupils should continue to attend lessons in which they are successful.

Referral panel

■ A referral panel, or similar systematic way of considering all referrals/requests for additional support for pupils, enables support staff to consider the scope of the intervention they can offer and the appropriateness for each individual pupil.

Exit criteria

■ Having clear exit criteria is as important as the entry criteria.

■ In order to be clear about the exit criteria we need to have a clear idea about what we aim to achieve.

Re-integration

Communication

■ Links with the pupil's tutor and Head of Year should continue throughout the intervention.

■ Liaising with other staff throughout the intervention is vital.

■ Regular contact with parents is an important element of the work of the LSU – who this contact will be through, i.e. Head of Year or LSU manager, should be negotiated and discussed.

■ Links with Learning Mentors, where they are part of the school's resources, is a valuable element of the approach.

Planning, monitoring and evaluating

■ We need to plan the pupil's return to mainstream lessons.

- High expectations of achievement should be maintained.
- The success of the re-integration needs to be monitored.
- Regular evaluation of the re-integration process will enable us to adjust our practice from an evidence base.

Suggestions for taking ideas forward

If you have not considered or used a referral panel model, a first step in reviewing entry, exit and re-integration might be to consider this model. If you already use this model, consider reviewing its effectiveness.

Questions you might need to answer include:

Who should be on the referral panel and what will they contribute to it?

Who can refer pupils to the panel?

What are the stages of support before the LSU and how is this support recorded?

What information is needed by the referral panel in order to make an informed decision about how to support individual pupils?

Is there a staged process of seeking information?

Is everyone clear about the stages of information giving and the reasons for giving the information?

What is the process for feeding back the decisions of the referral panel?

Are there parallel systems for reviewing individual casework and monitoring the success of interventions?

What is the process for re-referring a pupil to the panel?

Programmes within the LSU

- *What are the key Ofsted findings about programmes in LSUs?*

- *How does one emphasise learning and teaching within the LSU?*

- *How is an internal locus of control developed for both pupils and teachers?*

- *What programmes are used by existing LSUs?*

- *What are the range of therapeutic programmes on offer in LSUs?*

Introduction

Ofsted findings about LSU programmes

When planning the programme within the LSU it is important to bear in mind that the pupils who are referred for additional support will have complex needs. The LSU programme needs to reflect pupils' social, emotional and academic needs. A holistic approach is essential for the support of pupils to help them achieve their potential within a mainstream school environment.

Some key Ofsted findings mentioned in Chapter 1 reflected some of the issues we need to consider when planning the programme in the LSU:

> Too frequently, units focused on personal support at the expense of helping pupils to learn productively ... In a quarter of the units staff focused heavily on discussion about improving behaviour, at the expense of work on improving pupils' learning. Much of this discussion lacked focus and failed to follow basic counselling and support principles.
> (Ofsted 2003: 58, 60)

At the other extreme there are LSUs where pupils are sent to the unit with the work that they would have been doing in the classes from which they came, and each individual follows a specific and unrelated programme with no reference to others within the room. Both extremes are failing to use the flexibility and potential of the LSU provision. The pupils who are referred to the LSU need the time and opportunity to develop their interpersonal and social skills, and to reflect on the strategies needed to cope successfully within a school. They do also need to reflect on the main purpose of schooling, which is about teaching and learning.

Perceptions about exclusion

A recent research project (Riley and Rustique-Forrester 2002) looked at the differing perceptions of pupils, parents and teachers about factors which had led pupils to be excluded. When asking the pupils what makes a good teacher the main focus of the responses was about teaching and learning. Examples of the summary of attributes of good teachers included 'understanding and knowing the subject well', 'using a variety of teaching styles and innovative approaches' and 'willing to reward pupils for progress'. Clearly these teachers did have a positive relationship with pupils, but it was a relationship based around the teaching and learning process.

Another perception expressed by pupils within this research project was that once they were labelled as failures there was no chance of change.

> Many students expressed the view that once they, and other students, had got into a downward spiral of bad behaviour, exclusion and non-attendance, the chances of improving their prospects were almost nil
> (Riley and Rustique-Forrester 2002: 30)

Knight (1992) and Maines and Robinson (1988) discuss the concept of 'locus of control'. Knight reports:

> Students experiencing repeated failure have a lowered expectation of success, leading to underachievement and a belief that external factors control reinforcements. Any successes are likely to be attributed to external factors such as teacher help, luck, or easy task. An expectancy of failure for different behaviours in different situations is created. Feelings of powerlessness are generated leading to a generalised expectancy where reinforcements are viewed as being externally controlled and unrelated to personal behaviour.
> (Knight 1992: 164)

The description of an external locus of control seems to encapsulate in some detail the experiences and attitudes of many children with emotional and behavioural difficulties. The effects of maintaining an external locus of control could have a profound and far-reaching effect on a re-integration placement. It is essential that the pupil can assume responsibility for their own behaviour, and thus for their personal relationships. An internal locus of control, where responsibility and control for change are felt to rest within the individual, is essential for daily living and communication, as well as the motivation to learn and form relationships with others. 'We may hypothesise that externals are less likely to strive for achievements which they do not believe to be dependent on their own efforts' (Maines and Robinson 1988: 6).

LSU programmes

The programme within the LSU needs to reflect the needs of the individual pupils and also the wider role of the LSU manager. A clear emphasis on communication with parents/carers is necessary, including the programme, its aims, and the progress of their child on the programme. It needs to be made explicit to pupils and their parents/carers what the length of the intervention will be and how any re-integration will be supported and monitored.

An example of one specific programme is reflected in the case study below. The approach illustrated incorporates a holistic approach to emotional, behavioural and learning difficulties. The programme is made up of three main elements: specific strategies for working with pupils, training for staff, and support and strategy development for parents. The case study shows an example of a structured programme that a number of primary schools in Hammersmith and Fulham can access.

Case study: Summary of the Primary Learning Achievement Centre (Hammersmith and Fulham's Primary Learning Support Unit)

Aims of the Primary Learning Achievement Centre

- To reduce the number of pupils displaying emotional and behavioural difficulties in mainstream primary schools

- To reduce the number of fixed term and permanent exclusions from primary schools

- To support mainstream schools in the management of pupils who display emotional and behavioural difficulties

- To support children with their transition to secondary school

- To promote children's confidence and ability with their learning

Structure of the Primary Learning Achievement Centre

The Centre, based at Gibbs Green School, is in its fourth year of operation and is staffed by a teacher, learning mentor and part-time support assistant. The Centre is managed by the Link Learning Mentor for Hammersmith and Fulham.

Sixty pupils have attended the Centre since April 2000. Fifty-eight of these pupils have remained in their mainstream primary schools and avoided permanent exclusion. The Centre works with pupils in years 5 and 6 only. Seventeen Primary Schools in Hammersmith and Fulham can refer to the Centre. Pupils are transported to and from the Centre by the Centre's own car. Schools must complete a referral form for a place and Centre staff conduct a referral meeting at the beginning of each term to decide an appropriate cohort of pupils.

Pupils attending the Centre are supported for a period of ten weeks. Pupils are prepared for their attendance at the Centre by staff from the Centre visiting their schools prior to their placement. Pupils visit the Centre with their parents/carers before their placement so they feel more confident when they start. They attend the Centre for six weeks from Monday to Thursday, and return to their mainstream schools on Friday. There is a maximum of six pupils in the class. After their six-week placement, pupils return to their schools on a full-time basis and are supported for a further four weeks by the Centre's learning mentor and teacher. Centre staff support the pupil's class teacher and other relevant school staff in managing the referred pupil's needs and offer support with implementing Pastoral Support Plans, Individual Education Plans, setting up rewards and sanction systems and offering strategies to support the pupil's learning.

When pupils attend the Centre they participate in the National Literacy and Numeracy Strategies. Pupils have their own lap top computer and access to an interactive whiteboard; consequently they develop their Information Communication Technology Skills. On a daily basis pupils participate in circle time – a whole class discussion and listening forum. Skills and strategies are developed by pupils in the following areas: conflict resolution and anger management skills; concentration and listening skills; developing self-esteem; developing friendship and inter-personal skills; and developing skills to deal with secondary transfer. The learning mentor at the Centre is an accredited circle time trainer and has offered training to other learning mentors and school staff on circle time. In relation to pupils' learning and behaviour, the Centre teacher offers expertise in analysing pupils' learning styles and identifying pupils' barriers to learning. Consequently, some referred pupils had their learning or behaviour needs assessed by relevant professionals and some received statements to support their learning or behaviour. The Centre teacher meets regularly with class teachers to share successful strategies for supporting pupils and to review pupils' targets. Self-reflections and targets that pupils work on during their placement are sent to the pupil's school

(continued)

every week for their class teacher's attention. The Centre learning mentor works with pupils on their targets when they are attending their schools.

INSET offered to school staff who have pupils attending the Centre

Three INSET sessions are offered to mainstream schools' learning mentors, class teachers and Special Educational Needs Co-ordinators in relation to developing strategies to support referred pupils. These sessions are supported by an educational psychologist and focus on using solution focused brief therapy techniques to manage pupils. Additionally, school staff are given resources and strategies to manage the behaviour and learning of the referred pupils.

Parent support group

In conjunction with the Primary Pupil Referral Unit, also based at Gibbs Green School, the Centre offers a support group to parents/carers of current and past referrals. These sessions are led by a staff member from West London Action for Children. The sessions have been well attended and provide an opportunity for parents/carers to share their ideas and concerns with other adults experiencing the same difficulties. Furthermore, parents/carers reported that they learned strategies that helped them deal with the behaviour of their child in a more positive way. Staff from the Centre and Pupil Referral Unit attend some of the sessions. This provides the opportunity for staff to develop a greater understanding of the challenges faced by parents/carers in relation to managing their children.

Art project

The Centre was successful in bidding for the funding of an art project for a year. The art project, funded by the Gulbenkian Foundation and Education Arts Team from Hammersmith and Fulham Local Education Authority, has allowed a professional artist to conduct work with the Centre pupils for a year. The focus of the art project has been to increase pupils' emotional literacy in relation to secondary transfer. Additionally, the project gave primary and secondary learning mentors the opportunity to receive training on how to use art to promote pupils' emotional literacy. Learning mentors visited the Centre to observe the artist working with pupils to develop their own practice.

Autogenic training

During the summer term of 2003, pupils accessed autogenic training. The aim of this training was to teach pupils strategies to manage stress and improve relaxation skills. Pupils found the training beneficial in reducing the number of playtime incidents and enabled them to focus on their work more clearly, especially after playtimes.

Evaluation and assessment

A variety of data collection and assessment techniques are used to measure the impact of the Centre. Base-line assessment is used to record behaviours of referred pupils prior to their placement and when they re-turned to their schools on a full-time basis after their placement. Detailed reports are written by the Centre teacher and learning mentor. Pupils evaluate their own behaviour and learning using solution focused brief therapy techniques. Regular feedback from parents is made through telephone conversations or meetings.

(continued)

At the end of every term, school staff complete an evaluation form assessing the impact the Centre has made on improving the referred pupils' behaviour and learning. The following graph summarises the feedback given by schools using the evaluation form during 2001–02.

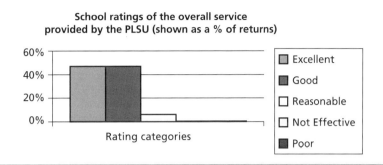

School ratings of the overall service provided by the PLSU (shown as a % of returns)

Programmes which offer input and support for both teachers and pupils are not common, but where they are used they seem to be very effective. The programme described above is highly structured and works with a small cohort of pupils for a set block of time, providing both centre-based intervention concentrating on academic and social skills and support within their mainstream schools during and after the programme. There are a range of different skills represented in the staff who work in the centre and they also utilise the expertise of supporting professionals when needed, for example when delivering solution focused training to school staff and support groups for parents. The centre has also been involved in an art project and trying alternative strategies for managing stress with the pupils accessing the support of the centre.

Below are outlined some brief examples of other types of approaches used.

Example A – primary linked unit

Primary pupils from two different schools access a unit based in one of the schools. There are targeted groups of pupils – approximately 12 per term (6 from each school) – who access the centre, half in the morning and half in the afternoon.

The LSU manager and one learning support assistant staff the unit. The schools are sufficiently close that staff from the LSU go to the other school site and collect and return the pupils at the beginning and ends of each session. This transfer routine is used as an opportunity to develop communication and social skills.

The pupils attend the half-day sessions at the LSU four days a week, and on Fridays the unit staff visit the pupils in their mainstream classes and have specific allocated time with class teachers and SENCo in the schools to discuss targets and progress. Whilst in the unit pupils have a mixture of literacy, numeracy and social skills games to develop their group work skills. Prior to commencement of the placement pupils are assessed using a behaviour baseline, and this is repeated at the end of the intervention.

Example B – secondary unit based in one school

Pupils in two year groups are targeted. The first are Year 9 pupils who have been having persistent problems throughout Key Stage 3 prior to the transition into Key Stage 4. There are two or three groups of six pupils who attend the LSU for one lesson per day. In this session they access social skills and anger management groups, set targets and discuss progress and strategies. The intervention usually lasts for half a term.

A further one or two groups of four pupils access more time in the centre. They attend the centre for some specific lessons and they complete a mixture of work – some is work from the lessons they are missing so that they do not fall behind, and some is extra work for additional lessons so that they can complete outstanding work or homework to get into a good work routine. This group may access the centre for longer than half a term and are also supported in some of their subject lessons by centre staff.

The other year group accessing the LSU are Year 7. This work is usually slow to start in the Autumn term, although some pupils highlighted at primary school receive immediate support from LSU staff in some lessons. Once the pupils who would benefit from support are identified the pattern is usually one of one lesson per day in the LSU, where pupils may receive a mixture of support for coping in a secondary school, social skills and group work sessions, and help with planning and completing class-based work and homework. The aim of the support is to avoid problems escalating later on.

The unit is staffed by one teacher and a learning support assistant, and the learning mentors in the school work closely with the centre manager to offer a range of support to pupils.

Example C – secondary unit based in one school

Pupils accessing the LSU attend for an average of one or more lessons per day for approximately one term, but this may be shorter if the pupils are coping well with other mainstream lessons.

The curriculum content of the LSU is varied and as well as the LSU manager some subject specialists teach specific lessons in the LSU. Subject teachers tend to be high profile teachers, for example Heads of Department and members of the Senior Management Team. Maths and literacy lessons are often taught by a subject specialist and also some art lessons. Teachers within the school are encouraged to visit the unit during the day and see pupils work. In addition, pupils present work or provide refreshments for invited teachers once every term.

Pupils from any year group can be referred to the LSU and although they are usually part of a group within the LSU, they may work with different pupils at different times of the day depending on the individual programme for each pupil. Pupils continue to attend lessons in which they are successful throughout their programme in the LSU, and are often supported by the LSU manager or a Learning Mentor back into less successful lessons.

Other units also concentrate on programmes aimed at short-term intervention for specific cohorts of pupils. Examples of programmes could include:

- Primary–secondary transfer preparation and post transfer support
- Programmes aimed at the transition from KS3 to KS4
- Re-integration programmes for pupils who are returning from a fixed term exclusion
- Re-integration programmes for pupils who have been out of school for some time (school refusers/phobics).

A research project about therapeutic LSU programmes

A research project in Nottingham, funded through an Excellence in Cities research grant, has been exploring what therapeutic programmes are on offer in LSUs across the city and how these programmes were perceived by LSU staff. These 'therapeutic services' include a combination of what the LSU is offering itself and additional services that are either provided by other agencies, for example CAMHS, or that the school 'buys in'. A number of different services can be offered by one provider (for example counselling and art therapy). In the second phase of the research the views of referrers (Heads of Year for example) and pupils themselves will be sought, to analyse their perceptions of which therapeutic services are the most effective. Some information about the project is shown below.

Mapping therapeutic services and approaches used by Nottingham City Learning Support Units

By Viv McCrossen and Saul Becker*

This paper summarises some of the key findings from the mapping exercise within Nottingham City LSUs (secondary schools), conducted as part of the *Therapeutic Approaches Project*.

Aims and background to the project

This project is concerned to:

■ Map the diversity of therapeutic service provision and approaches used with young people with behavioural difficulties in the Learning Support Units within all 18 Nottingham City secondary schools

■ Review the available research evidence on 'what works' and why

■ Consult with young people and their carers to determine their experiences of LSUs

■ Evaluate new therapeutic approaches used in Nottingham to try and identify models of good practice.

Method

The data presented in this summary were obtained in the course of interviews with Learning Support Unit (LSU) managers from all 18 secondary schools in Nottingham City. Each LSU manager provided details of their school and its overall experiences of using therapeutic services, and further details of *every* therapeutic service that their school made use of (including an assessment of the effectiveness of these services and the approaches that each service used).

Key findings

The study shows that 172 *therapeutic service provisions* are used by the 18 LSUs within Nottingham City secondary schools.

Referred behaviours

Aggression among secondary school pupils is the behaviour *most* frequently referred to a therapeutic service. Indeed, 23% of all reported service provision in Nottingham City involved aggression as the most referred behaviour.

Therapeutic approaches

Table 1 shows that counselling is used in 51 of the 172 service provisions. Put another way, *just under 30% of all service provision provides some form of counselling.*
    Additionally,

■ one quarter of all service provision provides some group work

(continued)

- one in five service provisions provide consultation
- 17% provide social skills training
- 11% provide anger management; *and so on.*

At the lower end of the Table, it can be seen that just under 2% of service provision contains some form of play therapy.

Table 1 Therapeutic approaches available through 172 service provisions

	Frequency	Percentage of service provisions (total = 172)
Counselling	51	29.7
Group work	43	25.0
Consultation	34	19.8
Social skills training	30	17.4
Activity based	26	15.1
Anger management	19	11.0
Family therapy	19	11.0
Psychological/psychiatric assessment	14	8.1
Parent training	12	7.0
Family resource workers	10	5.8
Brief solution focused	9	5.2
Learning support	9	5.2
Art/music/drama	6	3.5
Assessment/observation	6	3.5
Medical/medication	4	2.3
Play therapy	3	1.7
Other	23	13.4

The frequencies and percentages in Table 1 exceed 172 and 100% because each service provision can provide a range of therapeutic approaches.

Perceived effectiveness of the therapeutic approaches

All the approaches are viewed relatively highly, although some are rated as very effective/effective by a larger proportion of LSU managers than others.

The following approaches are ranked as *very effective* by the vast majority of LSU managers: anger management, learning support/mentoring, assessment/observation, medical/medication, play therapy, activity based, group work, social skills training, brief solution focused, counselling, art/music/drama therapy.

Approaches that are seen to be *most effective* are those where service providers offer a quick response rate, services are located within the school site or local community, services are accessible, and service providers communicate well with schools – keeping them informed of progress and developments.

Some highly valued services are in limited supply in Nottingham. These include, for example, art therapy, play therapy and brief solution focused work.

Early findings from follow-up interviews with young people who have used LSUs and therapeutic interventions suggest that what is important to them is their relationship with the therapist, having a safe and

(continued)

secure environment where the therapy takes place (which can include group work), and having time and space available to them on a planned or unplanned basis.

A full report will be published in 2004 providing details of the research, including the literature review.

---

* Viv McCrossen is project manager, Therapeutic Approaches Project, Nottingham City Education Department, Excellence in Cities. Professor Saul Becker is associate director, Centre for Child and Family Research, Loughborough University.

LSU managers within this research project valued speed of response and accessibility of services, and see these two aspects as key components in a programme's possible effectiveness. One of the additional questions that may need unravelling is whether it is the extra time or the specific intervention that is effective. Pupils' views may be the key to exploring this aspect of the survey, especially if they can give reasons why they felt a particular approach was more effective in their case.

Some key points covered in this chapter

- Communication between the school and the family, including the importance of good news and engaging the parents in the process of working with their child.
- A lively and challenging curriculum that meets the needs of the individual pupils.
- Good quality information and resources to meet individual needs at an academic as well as an emotional/social level.
- Including other staff as part of the programme in the LSU.

Some suggestions for taking ideas forward

If you are developing a programme in a new LSU or reviewing the programme in an existing LSU there are some key questions that need to be answered.

The group(s)

Who are the pupils in the target group?

Is it a specific year group?

Is it a transition focus?

Are there several target groups?

The timing

Once there is a group or groups of pupils you need to then decide:

What proportion of the day/week these groups will be accessing the LSU?

What proportion of the day/week they will be supported in mainstream lessons?

Who will offer this support?

What will the programme be?

What the programme will be will depend on the decisions you have made about the groups and the timing. For example, if you have decided that there are five different groups of pupils all accessing LSU support each day you may well be target setting and looking at learning skills or group skills, whereas if you have two groups accessing support both in and out of classes for 50 per cent of their school week you will be planning for more curriculum input and liaison with subject staff.

Recording, reporting, monitoring and evaluation

- *What are the aims and intended outcomes of the intervention?*

- *How does reporting vary for different audiences?*

- *How does evaluating enable the development of the LSU?*

- *How is monitoring achieved?*

- *How is recording carried out?*

Introduction

Before attempting to record, monitor and evaluate the intervention we need to be clear about:

- the aims of the intervention

- the length of the intervention

- the intended outcome of the intervention

- the intended systemic outcome of the intervention.

We also need to be clear about what are the agreed success criteria. These could include criteria related to:

- the individual pupil

- groups of pupils

- differences in staff approaches

- changes to whole school systems.

If we return to the review and planning spiral presented in Chapter 2 (page 9) this chapter illustrates part of the spiral in action. The processes described within this chapter keep the process of auditing, monitoring and evaluating part of the continued development of the LSU. Within the context of a whole school initiative the processes of negotiating and communicating with a variety of audiences about the work of the LSU also enhance the capacity of the work to influence the practice of other colleagues, and to affect positively the learning and teaching within the school.

Reporting

It is important to remember your audience when reporting either verbally or in written form. Possible audiences could include the Senior Management Team, school governors, other teachers, the LEA and the DfES. The format and content of the report would vary considerably depending on the audience. The timings of reports are also relevant when planning what the content of the report may be. Some reports have a specific format and there will be information that has to be included (see DfES reporting framework in Appendix 5, LSU Steering Groups). Reporting is also a forum for communicating and negotiating the work within the LSU, for example when reporting to the Steering Group, highlighting particular issues within your report can be a vehicle for generating discussion about possible changes in the provision. Seeing reporting as an opportunity to celebrate successes is one way of making it less burdensome. Reports can highlight what went well and what needs improving and will, if used in this way, be a useful tool.

Reporting should be easy if you have:

- clarified your aims
- carefully recorded the range of your work
- used effective monitoring procedures to inform your practice
- planned the evaluation of the LSU.

Include examples of good practice and case studies to illustrate the points made in your reports, and also examples of forms, letters and recording formats that you regularly use. Reports that include case studies and good practice examples (examples of actual work, with identifying names removed of course) are very effective and can bring the work of the LSU to life for those unfamiliar with the process, as well as being valuable tools for presenting information to others.

Reporting is useful if it is part of the monitoring and evaluation procedure. It is helpful if you can plan in to your procedures any annual or regular reports that you know you will have to write so that they do not become a last minute effort. Part of the set agenda for the steering groups in the schools I attend is a report from the LSU manager that follows the headings used for annual Excellence in Cities reporting. The purpose of introducing this framework was to enable managers to build their report during the year and just compile the elements at the end of the year for the 'official' report. Obviously different audiences require different types and amounts of information. Planning for the major reports and ensuring that this information is available and useful to you all year round is the most effective way to use the process.

Evaluation

Evaluating as described here is an ongoing process, but one that reflects on the implementation of an initiative or process over a period of time. We will not evaluate the impact of a programme in the LSU after one month, as it is likely the programme will be still in process and the impact will be difficult to measure. Evaluation after six months to a year, using the information we have gathered through our monitoring and recording procedures, is more realistic. Evaluation needs a clear focus and it is likely that monitoring and recording will be aimed towards the questions being asked as part of an evaluation. In other words, if they are working well the processes of reporting, evaluation, monitoring and recording are all interlinked.

It might be useful to reflect on recent advice to Ofsted inspectors about the suggested focus of an Ofsted inspection when evaluating the LSU. In new guidance to Ofsted inspectors the following framework is given:

In the unit evaluate:

- how well the teaching meets the identified needs of the pupils, taking into account their past performance;
- how well the staff provide pupils with strategies that work in practice;
- whether target setting is realistic and clear to pupils;
- links with parents, other agencies and education providers;
- the unit's assessment and record keeping; and
- the school's assessment of the impact of the unit and its use of information to improve work in the unit and in other lessons.

(Ofsted 2002: 10)

The last bullet point in the extract above is in some ways the most interesting. The implication is that what is required is evidence that the impact of the unit is not only on work in the unit but also in other lessons, and in order to improve the work in other lessons, there will need to have been effective changes in the behaviour and approaches of pupils and teachers alike. Without this whole school approach and impact the unit can only be partially successful.

Some examples of evaluating questions that you might find useful to explore are:

- Is the LSU part of a whole school approach to managing challenging behaviours?
- What evidence is there of systematic change as a result of the LSU initiative?
- Is the LSU making a difference?
- To whom is it making a difference?
- How do you know?
- Is this quantifiable?
- Whose views are being sought?
- How is this data being collected?
- Who is evaluating the LSU?
- How will this information be used to further develop the provision?

The following case study explores the way that one LEA co-ordinated the evaluation of the LSU initiative across schools, using a peer support process.

Case study: A participative approach to evaluating LSU provision

Context of the evaluation programme

Waltham Forest is a phase one Partnership and secured funding for LSU provision in 1999. Waltham Forest LEA is managed by EduAction.*

Prior to the recruitment of the EiC team in 2002, support for and monitoring of LSU provision had not been carried out systematically. Anecdotal evidence suggested that schools place a high value on their LSUs' contribution to the improvement of attendance, behaviour and increasing inclusive learning opportunities. However, there was little hard evidence to help evaluate their effectiveness. Discussions with Heads revealed that each school had developed a model to suit particular circumstances. Understandably, this resulted in considerable variation in provision.

In order to properly evaluate the LSU initiative, the EiC Partnership ratified a formal programme of LSU evaluations, to be carried out in the Autumn term of 2002 and the Spring term of 2003. The aim of this programme was to identify strengths in the quality of provision, suggest areas for development and strategies to secure improvement.

(continued)

Programme design

To ensure validity and impartiality of judgements, a team of four undertook the evaluation of each LSU:

- The EiC manager
- The Strand Co-ordinator for Learning Mentors and LSUs
- The Head or senior manager of another school
- The LSU manager of another school

In effect, each school was part of an evaluation and subject to another. Part of the programme design was to share practice and create professional development opportunities for LSU managers.

The evaluation programme was designed to be formative and developmental. As part of the process, answers to the following questions were sought:

- What is the relationship between the intended and actual aims, working practices, and outcomes of the LSU?
- What are the successes of the initiative and what are the areas for development?
- Is the LSU meeting its objectives?
- Is there equality of opportunity and access?

To ensure consistency of approach and that the programme was in keeping with national evaluation criteria, observation and interview schedules were developed in eight categories, using the DfES Audit Instrument (2002b). A Code of Conduct, adapted from the Ofsted Handbook, was also published.

Each LSU evaluation was timetabled around documentary analysis, observation in the LSU and a series of six discrete interviews with the Head, line manger of the LSU manager, LSU manager, other significant member(s) of staff in the LSU, mainstream teacher(s) and pupil(s). An optional seventh interview could be arranged with parents and carers of pupils in the LSU, at the school's discretion. At the end of the evaluation, the team provided verbal feedback to the Head.

Following the evaluation, each Head received a confidential written report analysing the evidence in each of the eight categories, identifying strengths of the provision and making recommendations for areas of development.

Prior to the series of evaluations, the EiC manager and strand co-ordinator met with Heads and/or senior managers, and the strand co-ordinator met with LSU managers, to discuss and consult on the programme design, code of conduct, audit instrument and interview and observations schedules. At the end of the process, the strand co-ordinator wrote a full evaluation report, analysing trends and themes across the programme of evaluations and making recommendations for developments. The emerging picture of LSU provision in Waltham Forest secondary schools is that of an increasingly efficient, well-focused and highly valued initiative.

Building on good work

To ensure that the process was developmental, the programme included the establishment of a series of LSU managers' network meetings, which culminated in a 'Development Day', to share best practice and take forward recommendations. A consultant trainer was commissioned to work with the strand co-ordinator to take forward common themes and areas for development.

Ways forward

Drawing on the programme of evaluations and the recommendations in the evaluation report, a Monitoring, Evaluation and Quality Assurance Strategy has been produced for 2003–04, with the aim of informing school improvement.

(continued)

The main thrust of our evaluation activity will be ensuring that LSU provision is fully integrated with whole school behaviour policy and practice. LSU managers will work with Lead Behaviour Professionals (identified within the Key Stage 3 Behaviour and Attendance Strategy) to undertake a comprehensive audit of behaviour across the school, and a review of behaviour policy. Each LSU manager will be asked to undertake a small developmental pilot project under the heading: 'What can be done to improve the effective contribution of the LSU at whole school/systemic level?' This will focus on the training and promotion of teaching behaviours and how to teach behaviour for learning skills. These developmental pilot projects will be a first step towards achieving a balance among pupil-focused work, whole school professional development activities and policy development.

* EduAction is a new organisation created to deliver key services of the highest quality to the schools in the London Borough of Waltham Forest.

The approach detailed in this case study looks at a range of views about the LSU and how it is meeting its objectives. The use of senior staff from another school ensures that good practice is shared between schools, and that across the LEA the LSU initiative is discussed and reflected upon. The use of an LEA representative (in this example both the EiC manager and the LSU strand co-ordinator) also ensures sharing of any good practice, and can be used to inform and develop training for individual schools and across the LEA. LEA co-ordination will be further explored in the following chapter.

Monitoring

Monitoring is part of the process for both reporting and evaluating. Within the spiral of systemic reflection and change, monitoring tends to focus on an aspect of the initiative – for example, a pupil's progress – and will form part of the evidence for an evaluation or a report. The focus of the evaluation will dictate part of the recording process and also what is to be monitored. What is monitored can also be used as a basis to inform others (governors, senior management, parents, school staff, outside agencies) about the work in the LSU. This sort of information can also be useful if you want to present a case to the steering group (see Appendix 5), as part of the evidence in the report, for example, for changing the way the programme in the LSU is run, or when asking for support or input in the LSU from other members of staff.

There are three key features: what is being monitoring, how it is being monitored, and by whom it is being monitored. For example, if you are monitoring the effectiveness of a particular approach with a group you will need to decide how you do this and who else might need to be informed/involved. However, if you are being monitored (or the effectiveness of the LSU is being monitored) by someone else, you need to be clear about how this is being done and how you will be informed of the information gained by this process.

Monitoring of the success of re-integration of individual pupils and the process of re-integration from the LSU is vital. We need to develop an effective process by learning from both successful and less successful re-integrations. This information can also be used in working with individual teachers and in developing staff training on effective ways of working with challenging pupils. It is often the case that strategies that are effective with challenging pupils will also be effective for all groups of pupils.

An in-school steering group for the LSU, as mentioned previously, is one way of both monitoring the progress and effectiveness of the LSU initiative, and ensuring that the LSU stays firmly on a whole school agenda.

Monitoring the perceptions of parents, pupils and other staff is very important to the work in the LSU. The success of the interventions with pupils will be affected directly by the perceptions of all these groups. The following case study and related appendix (Appendix 4) look at the approach of one group of LSU managers to gathering this information.

Case study: Eliciting pupils' views about a Learning Support Unit

Background

Learning Support Units are an 'in-school' provision that aim to support pupils with challenging behaviour. They aim to provide short-term provision designed to meet the pupil's individual needs, with an emphasis on positive prevention. Pupils are referred to the unit with clear criteria for entry and exit to and from the provision. Typically pupils are encouraged to reflect on their behaviour and, through this process, develop targets to focus on. However, pupils may also access specific programmes to support them with managing their behaviour. It is hoped that pupils will learn strategies to help them to manage the mainstream classroom, and they will be able to attend classes successfully over time.

Monitoring and evaluating the impact of the LSU as an intervention can be challenging due to difficulties with measuring changes within any system. Issues with quantifying behaviour can be amongst the most difficult unless a clear baseline is used. However, is it possible to measure pupil's perceptions of their progress, and this may help to indicate what aspect of support in the LSU they found particularly helpful. This has been highlighted as desirable in *Good Practice Guidelines for Learning Support Units* (DfES 2002c). This has also been recently raised as an area for consideration in HMI monitoring of LSUs (in *New Developments in the Secondary Curriculum* (Ofsted 2002).

Staff who manage the Learning Support Units in secondary schools in the borough meet each term. Through these meetings a collective decision was taken that a focused area of work for the next few terms would be to elicit pupils' views regarding the type of support they had received. This would be done through a questionnaire that could be given to pupils who had involvement from the intervention.

Questionnaires to elicit pupils' perceptions about the LSU

The questionnaires were devised according to key areas the LSU managers wanted to address in the LSU. These were broadly as follows:

- the pupil's perceptions of the purpose of the intervention

- parents' perceptions of the type of support their child had received

- which aspects of the intervention were supportive to pupils?

- how could any improvements be made?

The group then generated questions that could be asked within these areas (pupil, staff and parent questionnaire examples are included in Appendix 4). Questions for the pupil questionnaire were then selected to ensure that a range of questioning styles was used, including open/closed questions, forced choice responses and scaling techniques.

The Pupil Perception Questionnaire was initially given to Year 9 pupils who had recent involvement from the LSU. The pupils filled the questionnaire out independently, although a member of staff was on hand to support them if needed. Initially feedback was sought from the pupils, not only about their perceptions of the LSU intervention, but also about the process of filling in the questionnaire. It is hoped that the questionnaire will eventually be circulated to all pupils who spend time in the LSU, and analysed to determine which aspects of the support they found helpful. This information can then be used to inform the type of support that is offered in future.

Effects of careful monitoring might mean changes in detail or more fundamental changes to the LSU intervention. Monitoring the work enables flexibility and the use of evidence to justify any changes to the action plan.

Recording

In all schools there are numerous ways that information is recorded. One of the problems is that often staff are unclear about their aims and objectives and hence do not have a record to hand that can show clear evidence of improvement or progress from these objectives. Depending on the aims of the intervention or piece of work you may need a selection or all of the following types of records.

- Referral forms and information from the initial record of the intervention
- Notes from meetings with pupils, parents and other staff
- Notes from class observation
- Records of group activities and individual pupil participation
- Records of academic work and progress
- Records of re-integration progress
- Notes from work with staff either individually or in groups
- Records of pupils' view and opinions
- Records of changes to systems or processes whereby systems are reviewed.

Once the objectives and aims of a piece of work are clarified it is also beneficial at the outset to decide what records are to be kept, with clear reasons about why those records are needed and to what use they will be put. For example, if we are going to ask pupils for their views on the effectiveness of a programme or type of intervention, we need to use this information to inform planning for this pupil/group and further pupils/groups. Or if we are keeping notes of classroom observations, this is because these will be used either to feedback and work with individual teachers or groups of teachers, or because this will inform our work with pupils or be used in giving feedback to their parents.

Recording effectively enables monitoring, evaluation and reporting to be clear and evidence based. Communicating and negotiating with other staff about pupils and their needs becomes active professional development if it based on evidence clearly and purposefully collected and presented as part of an evaluation cycle.

Some key points covered in this chapter

- Reporting will be different depending on the audience it is for. Planning annual reports and building up to them through the year is helpful.
- Evaluating the work of the LSU needs to reflect how the unit is part of a whole school initiative and how objectives set are being met.
- Monitoring is most useful when it informs and develops the good practice in the LSU.
- Recording needs to reflect the variety of work going on in the LSU and should be planned to help with reporting needs.

Suggestions for taking ideas forward

Using the processes described within this chapter, discuss within the steering group for the LSU the existing processes and practice within the school for reporting, evaluating, monitoring and recording.

Are there aspects of the process that could be improved?

Do you have a clear timetabled reporting framework?

Are the areas that you wish to evaluate this academic year explicit?

Which aspects of the LSU provision are you currently monitoring and how is this being done?

What recording is currently undertaken and to what use is this information put?

How do you use the evidence you collect to communicate with other staff about the needs of the pupils and the work of the LSU?

From the answers to these questions develop an action plan for improving the process of collecting evidence and communicating the findings with others.

LEA co-ordination and support

- *How is an LEA database set up?*

- *What specific training is needed by LSU managers?*

- *What help can be given for primary–secondary transfer?*

- *How can LSU managers be supported?*

Introduction

The activities that an LEA can co-ordinate will vary, but some examples explored in this chapter include:

- The setting up and co-ordination of an LEA-wide database

- Specific training for LSU managers

- Helping schools across an LEA with the primary–secondary transfer process

- Regular network sessions for LSU managers to share good practice and facilitate the dissemination of up-to-date information relevant to managers and schools implementing the initiative

The LEA has an important role to play in providing advice and consultation, support and training for schools in the implementation of the LSU initiatives, and also specifically for LSU managers so that networks can be set up and maintained. The LSU initiatives have not been supported in the same way as the Learning Mentors, for example, under EiC; there has been no national training or expectation that LEAs would appoint a lead representative to ensure support for LSU managers. Within non-EiC areas the number of LSUs has been fewer and funding often short term and insecure. LSU managers report feeling unsupported and unrecognised nationally. However in some LEAs there has been very effective and targeted support for LSU managers through network sessions, training programmes and initiatives that aim to bring LSU managers together, sometimes with other colleagues from schools, i.e. Learning Mentors, to develop good practice for supporting pupils with challenging behaviours.

The setting up and co-ordination of an LEA-wide database

The idea of setting up an LEA database with information about the effectiveness of interventions within schools, allows dissemination of both individual schools' successes and also the impact of specific interventions across an LEA. It would, for example, be possible for an intervention to be effective in one school but not across an LEA. From this evidence questions could be posed about the strategies used in the successful school which could have a positive practical impact on other schools.

In Hounslow there is a dedicated full-time Lead Learning Mentor and a full time LSU co-ordinator. This has allowed the LEA the opportunity to develop an initiative aimed at helping schools to produce evidence to indicate the success of the LSU and learning mentor strands, and also to enable LEA staff to work with school staff to disseminate and enhance existing good practice across schools in the LEA.

Learning Support Units – Database Development – Hounslow

Setting the scene

The Excellence in Cities Plan was published in March 2001, and included initial plans for seven schools to be funded through EiC to develop on-site LSU provision, each linked with another school as a partner. The priority for the Partnership was inclusion, providing flexible support in attractive and well-resourced centres on-site. The schools wanted to develop group or individual programmes allowing pupils to maintain a place at their school. It was important to minimise disruption, provide a focused programme of curriculum and behavioural support for pupils experiencing difficulty, and to re-engage disaffected pupils and re-integrate them into lessons so they could work towards recognised accreditation upon completion of their school life.

As the LSU funding was linked with the EiC initiative the DfES required an Annual Report for each strand, with details of the impact of EiC across the authority, how it was addressing the needs of the 'at risk' groups identified, and how it could be developed in the future.

In January 2002 an audit of the LSU strand was undertaken, with a report presented to the Partnership in April. The audit was able to provide an overview of each LSU within its own school, and helped to identify areas for development and training. But it was unable to present hard data to prove that the EiC criteria were being addressed or what the impact of the individual strands was. Staff were saying that pupil attendance had improved or that behaviour was improving but had no evidence to show either in school, or to the Partnership.

April 2002 saw the launch of the Good Practice Guidance, which gave a clearer idea of what information should be gathered in order to plan an appropriate programme for an individual. The NFER and EiC Bid were also revisited to see what would be required for school, local and national evaluation of the LSU strand. Following this, information was gathered from the Pan London LSU meetings, and colleagues who had been in the first Phase of EiC. We were then able produce a list of data that would provide evidence of improving attendance, achievement and behaviour in the summer of 2002.

Data collection strategies and problems

Between April and September 2002 the Link Learning Mentor and the LSU Strand Co-ordinator worked together to develop a data collection system that would serve both strands, because we did not want to duplicate data collection in schools. There are so many common areas, and in schools where there are both LSU and LM strands in place they are working together to provide a continuum of support for pupils, and often pupils receive support from both strands during a term.

We produced a spreadsheet to collect information from all LSU and LM schools in the authority, to be used in September 2002. This would require the leaders of each strand to provide information on individual pupils, much of which should have been in pupil profiles but needed to be transferred to the collection sheet.

The LSU managers were kept informed of developments, as were the schools' EiC managers and the Partnership Heads. It was important that we gave plenty of time for staff to input the first set of data and have

(continued)

access to IT support if they required it. We have also encouraged EiC managers to work with the schools' data managers to develop a system that will make data input as efficient as possible. Fields such as target grades for SATs can be entered by admin or other department staff if the spreadsheet is on the staff central system without confidentiality being breached. This will also make more staff aware of the support some pupils they teach are receiving, and hopefully raise awareness that they have a part to play in supporting pupils experiencing difficulties.

During this term we explored the possibility of importing centrally held data, and spent time talking with the Research and Statistics department of the local authority to see how much they could do. They said it would in future be possible to supply all centrally held information for individual pupils, provided they had either a UPN or the pupil's Forename, Surname and Date of Birth, and this could done using Excel Spreadsheets for collection.

This means that we will be able to reduce the amount of information that a school has to provide. But we also want to make sure that the individual pupil information is complete for the LSU and LM staff, so it was agreed that we would provide complete records back to the schools when the system had been tested and was fully operational.

The Data Administrator has always been available to support strand leaders and has, during the year, provided training for all LSU and LM staff in the schools and provided guidance on completing the spreadsheet. Written guidance has been produced for the schools, and the data sheets colour-coded following the trial at the beginning of the Autumn 2002 term, to let schools know what information we could now provide centrally.

Use of data

The first set of data collected covered the first half term of the 2002 Autumn term, and has provided the local authority and schools with a set of baseline data. Even though the planning and preparation was thorough we were unable to collect full data from each school with an LSU. There were difficulties collating data due to staff changes, and the fact that LSUs were still in a very developmental stage for some schools, one of which had only just appointed a manger in the September of 2002.

We did, however, get full data from five of the seven schools and the majority of data from one other. Only one school was unable to supply any data in the first round. It was possible from this data to produce a report for the EiC Partnership before the end of the Autumn term, showing that attendance was being improved by the introduction of LSUs.

Key Stage 4 attendance had increased by 1.55 per cent, and Key Stage 3 by 0.38 per cent for the identified pupils during the half term. Combined with the verbal responses it was now possible to show that one school had improved the attendance of a Key Stage 4 group by 15 per cent during the period the data was collected for. This information was given to the school, and provided valuable information on the effectiveness of the initiative during an inspection the following term.

It was also noted that one school had reduced attendance for a Key Stage 4 group of about 10 per cent, but we were then able to look at the referrals made by the school to the LSU, and noted that this was due to one or two pupils who had not been attending school regularly since Year 7, and who had never attended the LSU. It was then possible to review the referral procedures, and where it was felt a placement in the LSU would be beneficial to re-integrate the pupil the Educational Welfare Officer worked with the family or pupil before a placement was confirmed. This helped the school to make best use of the support available to each pupil, and made sure that places were not left unfilled because of inappropriate referral to the LSU.

We were also able to check that schools were supporting the pupils identified as at risk for a variety of reasons, and not just being referred pupils that wouldn't behave, or who had learning difficulties and were difficult to include in some lessons. There were 115 pupils registered with an LSU during this period; only 7.82 per cent had full Statements, with 36.5 per cent receiving no support other than LSU placement. Those who did have statements were able to continue working with the learning support departments, at the same time as receiving support to address behavioural or emotional difficulties.

(continued)

It is important that we not only look at the short-term impact of EiC initiatives on pupils, and schools, but that we track pupil progress following exit from the LSU placement. LSU staff were aware that pupils may be re-referred, and that some would require minimal support, or onward referral to more appropriate placements, following their exit from the LSU. If this support were not available then all the progress made could be undone. Therefore it is also important that this follow-up provision can be made available in school, or from other agencies. The information we gather during the next year about onward referrals will help the schools and support agencies develop planned focused support activities for some pupils.

The first full trials of the database will begin with the collection of the July 2003 spreadsheets from schools, which will complete the data for the 2002–03 school year. The Data Administrator will input the information, and provide reports on all fields by September 2003. The Partnership Heads will receive all reports as an overview, and where possible compared with reports for the whole school population of Hounslow. They will also receive the reports for their own school compared to the overview. We hope that they will use this data to celebrate success, and develop the work of the LSU in their own school.

With the implementation of the New Ofsted Inspection Framework in September 2003, when schools will be providing evidence of Self-Evaluation and Review, it is expected that this will provide schools with the data they need to prove that the EiC initiatives are effective in supporting pupils at risk in their school. Coupled with the Audit and Planning Documents that will be used across the LSUs from September 2003, it is hoped that LSU staff will be able to plan for individuals and groups, LSU managers and Heads will be able to share and embed good LSU practices within their own establishments, and the Strand Co-ordinators will be able to provide appropriate and focused support for LSU and Partner Schools across the authority.

The database, although initially problematic to set up, will provide schools and the LEA with evidence on which to base appropriate and focused support for pupils within a school as well as for schools within the LEA. A tool such as a database that can provide information at both school and LEA level which will aid planning and the sharing of good practice, is a valuable development.

Specific training for LSU managers

Another example of an approach used by a number of LEAs is the development of either a programme of training specifically for LSU managers, or the offering of individual days of appropriate INSET.

Examples of the types of programmes offered include:

- Child development and the psychological basis for specific approaches to behaviour change. For example, behaviour modification is based in a specific model of child development theory, and understanding the basis of this theory will enable practitioners using these approaches to understand the strengths and limitations of them and adapt them accordingly. Other approaches considered could include cognitive theory, social learning theory, psychodynamic theory, etc. The aim of the programme is to give managers a better understanding of the strategies they may be applying, enabling them to use them more discerningly, to understand why they work or fail and to disseminate this information to other staff so they too can apply a range of strategies and approaches if appropriate.

- Approaches to working with staff. Working with LSU mangers to develop effective ways of working in someone else's classroom, feeding back after an observation, disseminating strategies that work, running an INSET session, effectively communicating and negotiating with the whole school, etc.

- Solution focused brief therapy. The theory and practical implications for working with staff and pupils; developing ideas together for adapting the approach in different settings.

- Counselling skills appropriate to use with pupils in the LSU.

- Recording and reporting for different audiences.

- Monitoring, evaluating, recording and reporting.

- Preparing for an Ofsted inspection.

There are of course many other examples across the country of INSET offered to LSU managers, but the feedback from any sessions I have run suggests specific training is needed for the role and the practice of running and managing an LSU. Whilst the DfES have indicated that they are developing a programme that can be used for LSUs, this has been a long time coming. The programme developed by LEAs for local needs and with local LSU managers may well continue to be the best way forward. For LEAs newly developing this initiative the best place to start is with the identified training needs of the LSU managers in post. As the range of jobs for professionals to work with challenging pupils has developed, so the pool of experienced and qualified personnel has diminished. Many newly appointed managers are very keen and dedicated but they need appropriate support and training; if this is provided at an LEA level we will perhaps ensure a widening rather than a diminishing pool of effective and confident professionals.

Helping schools across an LEA with the primary–secondary transfer process

The transition from primary to secondary school is a very stressful and uncertain time for all pupils. For pupils with social, emotional and behavioural difficulties it is essential that this transfer is supported as effectively as possible. Many LSUs at primary schools are targeted at Year 5 and 6 pupils, and increasingly secondary LSUs have specific groups of vulnerable Year 7 pupils. Co-ordinating effective practice across the transfer process is a potentially valuable boost to the chances of successful transfer for some pupils. The case study below illustrates an example of an approach to encourage the transfer of information and support for vulnerable pupils across one LEA.

Case study: Primary–secondary transfer meeting framework

Aim: To exchange information on vulnerable Year 6 pupils transferring to Hammersmith and Fulham Secondary Schools

Relevant for: Primary and Secondary Learning Mentors, Learning Support Unit Staff and Year 7 Heads of Year

Time	Agenda items
2.00–2.10	Primary staff signing up for sessions to meet with secondary staff Tea, coffee and refreshments

(continued)

2.10–2.25	Case Study by Terry Debney (LSU Manager, Fulham Cross School) and Yvette Unsworth (PLSU Manager and Link Learning Mentor) on working together to support a vulnerable pupil successfully transferring to Fulham Cross School
2.25–2.35	Exploring the issues hindering successful secondary transfer for vulnerable pupils
2.35–2.45	Ways forward
2.45–4.30	Primary learning mentors and LSU staff sharing information with secondary staff about vulnerable pupils from their primary schools transferring to Hammersmith and Fulham Secondary Schools

Primary learning mentors were asked to complete a form prior to attending the meeting so they had a summary of information to hand to secondary staff about the vulnerable pupils they were discussing.

Below is an example of a booking sheet for primary mentors to meet with secondary staff. They booked 3–4 sessions/time slots.

Bookings with Henry Compton staff

Time	Name of Primary School Contact Person	Name of Primary School
2.45–2.50		
2.50–2.55		
2.55–3.00		
3.00–3.05		
3.05–3.10		
3.10–3.15		
3.15–3.20		
3.20–3.25		

Over forty people attended the meeting from 20 schools.

Collation of results from brainstorming activity on things hindering successful secondary transfer for vulnerable pupils

- Lack of communication between primary and secondary schools
- Lack of quality time to meet and discuss vulnerable pupils transferring
- Ineffective timing of transfer of information, leaving it too late
- No clear system of transferring information
- Lack of parental involvement
- Repetition of curriculum in Year 7
- Lack of understanding of people's roles in supporting secondary transfer
- Primary staff not knowing the most relevant person to contact at secondary schools and not being able to make contact with the person
- Negative labelling can hinder a fresh start
- Primary staff not knowing enough about the nature and structure of secondary schools

(continued)

Collation of main themes on ways forward in supporting vulnerable pupils with secondary transfer

- Transfer of information and visits need to be done as early as possible
- Have a named worker in secondary and primary schools to co-ordinate transfer
- A borough-wide timetable of enrolment and induction days, etc. to be disseminated to key staff and parents
- A borough-wide clear process where staff know how and when information is transferred
- More parental involvement in the transition process, involving the pupil, facilitated by primary and secondary mentors working together
- Maintaining transition links between primary and secondary staff after transition
- Lots of preparation work with pupils at primary level, to include the themes of ending and change
- Observation and dissemination of good practice in regard to supporting pupils with transition
- Honest open and fair communication of pupils' predicted performance in secondary schools, but without negatively labelling pupils

Evaluation of primary–secondary transfer meeting completed by participants

When asked how effective the meeting was in supporting vulnerable pupils transferring to secondary schools the results were summarised as:

Percentage (%)	Category
82	Very effective
18	Effective
0	Not effective
0	Not sure
0	N/A

Comments made by participants were

'An excellent opportunity to discuss concerns and make contact with secondary staff. Also a good time to arrange visits face to face – this can be difficult to arrange over the phone!' (Primary Learning Mentor)

'I now have a good idea of which students I can put into our different support groups, e.g. Success Maker, Literacy Support, Nurture Group and Peer Mentoring.' (Secondary Transition Co-ordinator)

Suggested action points

- Holding the meeting as early as possible once secondary places are allocated
- To involve Year 6 teachers
- A longer meeting to incorporate successful transfer practice and case studies

The approach outlined in the case study allowed professionals from primary and secondary schools to share information and to reflect upon the importance of communication for the successful transfer of vulnerable pupils. The majority of participants found the meeting very effective, and they were encouraged to plan for further improvements in a future meeting.

Regular network sessions for LSU managers

As well as training designed to develop the role of the LSU manager, another important role the LEA can play is in the co-ordination and facilitation of regular network sessions. These probably need to take place at least once a term so that professionals, who can feel rather isolated, get an opportunity to discuss relevant issues with colleagues regularly. In some LEAs the line managers of LSU managers are also invited to these network sessions. The attendance by line managers allows for opportunities to present activities, new guidance or initiatives to be discussed and reflected upon within a facilitated context. It also allows line managers to hear about practice in other schools and to think about varying models of implementation. If individual schools are also regularly allowed access to an LEA representative who has an overview of the LSU initiative, these ideas can be developed and discussed within the steering groups at the individual school level.

Examples of the type of areas covered in network sessions are:

- Sharing of good practice in a particular area, for example re-integration or the development of a referral panel model.

- Looking at reporting formats and agreeing as a group areas for development to be reviewed at further meetings.

- Considering and sharing whole school approaches to behaviour management.

- Communication with other staff – workshop approaches to developing alternative strategies.

- Using a solution focused meeting format to consider individual case studies and gather suggestions from colleagues.

- Presentation of new DfES or Ofsted guidance or initiatives, with time to reflect on the implications for LSUs.

These are some examples, and there are many more. The main aim in bringing managers together is to offer the opportunity for dissemination and sharing of good practice, to ensure that they are up-to-date with new initiatives locally and nationally, and to offer the space and time to reflect on and try different strategies with supportive colleagues. A typical agenda might include:

- Update on any national initiatives and documents relevant to the LSUs

- Update on any local initiatives relevant to the LSUs and the pupils accessing the provision

- Sharing of a particular area of good practice, followed by discussion and possible action planning in working groups

- Brainstorming or collaborative problem-solving on a particular issue or problem

Some key points from this chapter

The LEA has an important role to play in facilitating the networking and training of LSU managers.

Dissemination of good practice is a key part of this role.

An LEA co-ordinator can initiate strategies for enhancing the work of the LSU, for example primary–secondary transfer meetings and collection of key data across the LEA.

Suggestions for taking ideas forward

If the LEA is starting to set up a co-ordinated approach to supporting LSUs some first steps include:

1   Visiting all the existing provision.

2   Asking LSU managers what support and training they have already accessed and what they feel they need.

3   Using this information, plan regular network meetings.

4   Using this information, plan appropriate training.

5   Offering to support in-school steering groups or promoting this type of model.

If the LEA has an established model of supporting LSU managers an evaluation of the perceived effectiveness of this support may be a valuable process. This includes:

■   Asking whether the existing balance of central and in-school support is considered helpful.

■   Surveying LSU managers on their present training needs.

■   Reviewing with LSU managers existing reporting frameworks and how useful these are.

As the support the LEA is seeking to provide should be based on the needs of the schools and LSU managers within these schools, constantly monitoring the effectiveness of the support offered is a vital component of all planning.

Appendix 1
Questions asked in staff interviews as part of the whole school behaviour audit

1   Were you involved in the formulation of the school's behaviour policy?

2   Do you feel you have a clear understanding of the policy?

3   Do you feel the majority of pupils understand and follow the school rules/expectations?

3a How are pupils who find it difficult to understand and follow the rules supported?

3b Do you actively *teach* pupils how to conform to the school rules/expectations?

3c How do you reward those who behave appropriately?

4   What rewards do you use to motivate your pupils?

5   What range of sanctions do you currently use in order of severity of the problem?

6   What strategies do you use to manage behaviour problems?

7   How do these strategies relate to the school's behaviour policy?

8   Do you feel pupils know the reasons behind the rules in the school?

9   Do you feel there is a collective responsibility for behaviour management in the school?

10 Do you feel confident to acknowledge difficulties?

11 Are there clear protocols for gaining help?

12 Do you feel staff have effective guidance in dealing with conflict?

13 How are you finding using the current logging system for good and poor behaviour?

13a Any suggestions for improvement?

14 How do you feel pupil behaviour could be improved across the school?

15 Does pupil behaviour tend to cause you stress?

16 How do you manage stress?

17 Would you welcome a Peer Support System as a whole school strategy for managing behaviour?

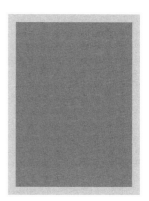

Appendix 2
Example of a referral form format

Pupil's name: Year: Class/Tutor group:

COP stage: CLA Y/N   CPR

What are the main areas of concern?

Behaviour   Attendance   Learning

Friendships   Relationships with adults   Unstructured time

How long have you had these concerns?

What strategies have been tried? By whom? For how long?

What were the outcomes of these strategies?

How have parents/carers been involved in the strategies tried?

Appendix 3
Teacher information sheet for solution focused meeting

Pupil's name: Class / Tutor group:

Please give a brief description of the behaviour that gives cause for concern at the moment:

Now take a moment to think of some of the times when you have noticed the pupil doing a bit better in class. These observations will be helpful as we try to develop some solutions to the current difficulties.

Please be specific. For example, 'Joan does better in class when she is on time for the lesson and when she is not sitting with her friends'.

1

2

3

4

Teacher signature: Date:

Please return this form before the meeting. Thank you for your help.

Appendix 4
Pupil, staff and parent perceptions of the LSU

(Compiled by LSU managers in Wandsworth as part of a network meeting on monitoring the impact of the LSU within school)

Pupil perceptions questionnaire	
What kinds of information would you like to know?	Questions that could be asked
Do pupils understand what the LSU is for?	■ What do you think is the purpose of the LSU? ■ Why do you think you were referred? ■ Write three words you would use to describe the LSU?
What has or what has not been effective/supportive?	■ What do you think has worked well? ■ What areas of your behaviour have improved, e.g. attendance / punctuality / attitude . . . ■ How has it helped you as a person? ■ Is there anything you feel has not worked well? ■ What could make it better?
Other perceptions	■ What do your parents think about the LSU? ■ What changes have your parents / teacher noticed with your behaviour? (Scale none to significant) ■ What did your friends think of the LSU? ■ Do you think your friends would do well if they came to the LSU? ■ Would you recommend the LSU to any of your friends who are finding school hard? (Yes / No)

Parents perceptions questionnaire	
What kinds of information would you like to know?	Questions that could be asked
Perceptions of the LSU	■ What do you think is the purpose of the LSU? ■ Why do you think your child was referred?
Impact or changes	■ What do you think has worked well? ■ What areas of your child's behaviour have improved, eg. attendance / punctuality / attitude . . . ■ Do you think your child has benefited from the programme? (Yes / No) ■ Have you seen any changes in your child's behaviour at home? ■ Has your child been positive about the LSU?

Staff perceptions questionnaire	
What kinds of information would you like to know?	Questions that could be asked
Do staff understand what the LSU is for	■ What do you think is the purpose of the LSU? – To help students to adopt better behaviour practices. – To help students to reflect on their behaviour and set targets for improvement. – To provide respite for the rest of the class. – To teach good behaviour. – To enforce a 'short sharp shock' regime. – Helping non-attenders to re-integrate. – A place where pupils can go to cool off. – Helping excluded pupils to manage their behaviour in the classroom. ■ Do you understand the criteria for referring pupils to the LSU? (Yes / No) ■ Do you feel you fully understand the purpose of the LSU?
What do staff see as their role / involvement / input to work at the LSU	■ What contact do you have with the LSU pupils? ■ Do you spend any time in the LSU? ■ What kind of support was offered to you as a member of staff when a pupil was re-ingrated back into lessons? – How effective do you feel this support was? (scale of 1 to 4) – What could have made it better? ■ How would you want to affect the operation of the LSU? – By teaching in the LSU? – By having access to the LSU for any pupils who need support? – By receiving regular feedback and giving updates?
How effective is the LSU?	■ What change have you noticed in pupils' behaviour on return to class? ■ Do you feel that time at the LSU has helped students, and how? ■ To what extend do you feel the LSU has contributed to the improvement of pupil behaviour in the school? (not at all to had a significant impact)

Appendix 5
Planning a new unit

When planning a new LSU provision there are a number of areas to consider, including:

- Establishing a steering group for the LSU
- The location within the school
- The learning environment
- Staffing
- Discipline
- Linked Units

Each of these areas will be developed in separate sections of this appendix. The sections are separated so that they can be photocopied and used as the basis for planning within the school. The order is a suggested order of progression, but it could be varied depending on the stage of planning that the school is at. For example if the appointment of the LSU manager is the first task then setting up the steering group would come second. In many schools the LSU is planned for and discussed before staffing positions are advertised and hence the order suggested here.

Establishing a steering group for the LSU

The establishment of a steering group for the LSU is one way of ensuring that the planning and monitoring of the unit within the school is seen as a whole school initiative from the outset.

Steering group membership

Staff involved in the steering group should include:

- a member of the senior management team
- the LSU manager (when appointed)
- learning mentors (or a representative)
- Heads of Year (or at least one representative for secondary schools) or a representative class teacher for primary schools.

The steering group may also include:

- the SENCo and other appropriate staff, depending on the pastoral system.

For units linked with another school(s), equivalent representatives from each school may be invited to the meetings (see section on Linked Units (page 87) for further discussion on this issue).

It is advisable to involve some outside support and advice at these meetings, which will add an additional perspective, such as an LEA representative, Behaviour Support Team representative, Educational Psychologist or other relevant person.

LEA links

An LEA co-ordinator could be involved in LSU steering groups across all participating schools. It is a very effective way of disseminating good practice between LSUs. Inevitably different schools employ different strategies and everyone can all learn from the successful practice of others as well as from their mistakes. Having input from someone from the LEA who attends a number of different steering groups is an effective method of support and of developing links between schools.

Purpose of the steering group

The purpose of a steering group is to support and promote the work of the LSU within the school or group of linked schools in which it is based. Part of its brief is to take a strategic overview for planning changes to the provision offered by the LSU when this is needed. Another element is evaluating outcomes for pupils that have accessed LSU provision so that good practice can be built upon.

Referrals to the LSU and discussion of the progress of individuals, is *not* part of the brief of the steering group. This should be dealt with in a different meeting (see referral panels, discussed in Chapter 4).

Format of a meeting

Prior to the establishment of the LSU, the steering group may meet quite frequently to discuss issues arising and formulate referral and communication arrangements. Once the LSU is established the steering group will probably meet about once a term. A useful standing item on the agenda is a report from the LSU manager, and this is most appropriately based around the format of any annual or regular reports that are needed. In this way the steering group is both informed of and can be supportive in the preparation of reports. A summary of successes and issues arising from the work in the LSU is also a useful starting point for discussions. Communication and feedback to the staff group and the senior management team can also be discussed and agreed at the meeting. Other issues the steering group will need to consider include:

- promoting a positive image of the work of the LSU
- any changes to the curriculum or programme in the LSU in the light of experience
- the re-integration of pupils from the LSU, the development of ideas and initiatives to enhance this process
- links with other in-school systems
- links with outside agencies
- communication with parents
- updating information sent out from the LSU to other agencies, parents and the rest of the school.

Reporting framework for the steering group

Reporting on a regular basis to the steering group using specific indicators helps LSU managers keep a track of relevant information.

The DfES issued a framework for reporting at the beginning of the Excellence in Cities initiative which in Wandsworth was further supplemented in line with DfES requirements for comprehensive quantitative data about LSUs. The first type of data was whole school data, which applied to all the Social Inclusion: Pupil Support strands, and is included in Box A5.1. The second type of data was specific to the LSU itself and is included in Box A5.2. Whilst not suggesting that this is the only framework that could be used, the information requested in these two sets of data offers a broad picture of what is happening in the school.

Using the headings in Box A5.2 or a similar framework as the termly report from the LSU manager to the steering group, offers a number of areas for discussion within the meeting. If the school has to report back to the LEA or the DfES on an annual basis using a specific framework, it is worth using this as the basis for the termly reports. In this way the annual report has written itself in the amalgamation of the three steering group reports.

Box A5.1   Social inclusion: Pupil support school targets and performance indicators

1. A reduction in the number of permanently excluded pupils
2. A reduction in the number of pupils on fixed term exclusions
3. A reduction in the number and frequency of incidents of particular types of behaviour that are a problem in the school
4. A reduction in non-authorised absences
5. A reduction in the number of pupils taken off roll for non-attendance or similar reasons
6. An increase in the number of permanently excluded or other off-roll pupils who are re-integrated full-time

7. An increase in the number of permanently excluded or other off-roll pupils who are re-integrated part-time through dual registration arrangements with the PRU

8. An increase in the number of pupils supported through dual registration with the PRU for school-based work to avoid exclusion or truancy

9. Evidence of improved educational attainment, behaviour and attendance of targeted pupils

10. Evidence of the improved effectiveness of whole school approaches to pupil inclusion

11. Evidence of satisfaction of school staff with the additional support provided and the effectiveness of the school project

---

Box A5.2 Performance indicators for each LSU

1 Total number of pupils accessing the LSU

2 Breakdown of length of time spent in unit by pupils (no. attending for less than half a term/ half a term/between one term and one and a half terms/between one and a half and two terms)

3 Breakdown of pattern of attendance at the unit – no. attending 10%, 20%, 30% . . . full-time/100% (where 10% = 1 half day session)

4 Number in KS3/ number in KS4

5 Boy/girl ratio

6 Ethnicity breakdown

7 Number of pupils successfully re-integrated fully into mainstream

8 Number of pupils successfully re-integrated partly into mainstream

9 Number of pupils accessing the unit subsequently permanently excluded or non-attenders

10 Evidence of improved behavioural attainments in relation to the baseline assessment and targets set out in the IEP or PSP

11 Evidence of improved educational attainments in relation to the baseline assessment and targets set out in the IEP or PSP

12 Nature and extent of LSU links with the Learning Mentors

13 Nature and extent of LSU links with Senior Staff

14 Nature and extent of parental involvement

15 Time spent by Unit staff in mainstream lessons monitoring current/past pupils accessing the Unit/observing potential pupils

---

The process of producing and presenting reports on the work of the LSU enables both outsiders and staff within the centre to reflect on the work of the LSU and plan for developments from an evidence base.

Location within the school

It is often the case that there is very little flexibility about the location of the LSU. However, it is worth exploring the pros and cons of the suggested location, and the reason for this is because this will help you to plan ways of overcoming any drawbacks. The ideal location may vary from school to school. It will not be tucked away in the furthest corner of the building where only those lost and unfamiliar with the school venture! However, if that it is the only space available (after genuine careful consideration of the disadvantages) there are ways of making it work. For example, if the space is used for other activities (clubs, meetings, etc.) at break and lunchtimes or even after school, other staff and pupils will be encouraged to venture there, especially if when they arrive they discover it is well equipped and welcoming in its appearance, with work displayed and a clear work focus!

Examples of LSU locations and how they might work

The LSU is at the very top of the school building or to one side where it is the only room accessed by a particular flight of stairs

In this scenario you could plan other uses for the LSU such as an after-school club or lunch-time drop in where any pupils can access support. You could also invite staff and pupils to view work or special projects completed in the LSU. Ensuring the room is bright, attractive and inviting will be essential as once people come in you want them to return.

In this scenario you could also timetable other staff to work with LSU groups, so that both staff and pupils saw this as an area where a number of staff taught. Another strategy for encouraging staff to use the space would be to hold re-integration meetings (like those suggested in Chapter 4) in the LSU, and provide refreshments.

The LSU is right in the middle of a busy thoroughfare where everyone walking past can look in

Blinds on the window would obviously help pupils to feel less like fish in a bowl. Planning the work in the LSU to take into account lesson change-over times or times of great movement (e.g. assembly time in a primary school) may help. For example, avoiding any intense group discussion work at this time would be useful.

Ensuring that the room looks inviting and attractive, with pupils' work displayed on the walls, may be beneficial. Anyone looking in as they go past can feel positive about the programme.

These are just a couple of examples but they illustrate the thought that can be given to enhancing both the image and appeal of the LSU, and making the pupils who access this support feel positive about the intervention.

Learning environment

Linked with location, the space provided for the LSU is not always ideal, but there are ways of thinking through the most appropriate and safe use of the space. Inevitably, to improve the environment for the specific purpose of an LSU will require some investment. The LEA may be able to help both financially and with advice.

Use of physical space

Room size needs to be considered and managed. If a room is too small it can force proximity and increase tensions within the group (Dwivedi 1993). In this case the size of groupings and how they might work together would need to be considered. If the room is too large this can also have drawbacks and inhibit participation of group members (Tessmer and Harris 1992). If the room is too large for the small groups that will be working in there it can be divided into different areas with screens and with furniture grouped to encourage different ways of working. Figures A5.1 and A5.2 show different layouts in a divided space.

In Figure A5.1 the space in the room is divided into two, with a group work table format and computer workstations in groups the other side of a dividing screen. This is an example of one way a larger space could be used.

Figure A5.2 shows a smaller area divided to provide similar flexibility.

The physical space needs to enable the pupils referred to the unit to feel safe and contained.

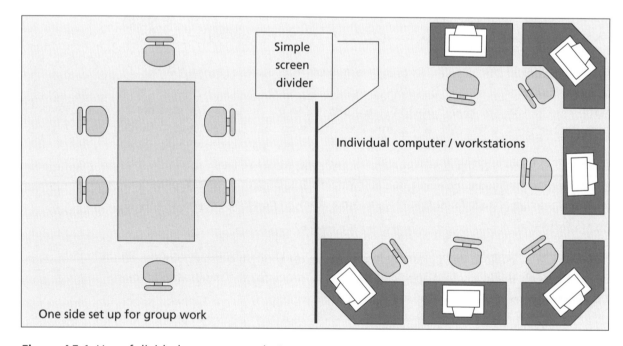

Figure A5.1 Use of divided space: example 1

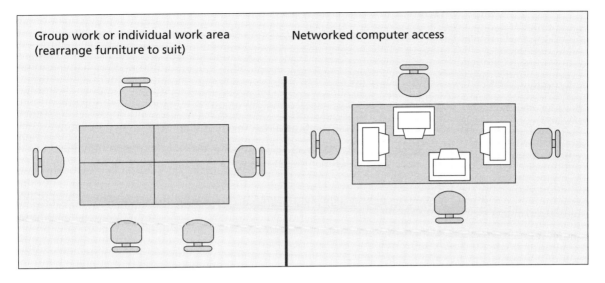

Group work or individual work area
(rearrange furniture to suit)

Networked computer access

Figure A5.2 Use of divided space: example 2

Noise levels and acoustics

Linked with the size of the room can be problems with acoustics. These can be minimised by the use of floor coverings (carpet or carpet tiles) and screens, which can help to absorb sound. If the noise problems are associated with the area outside the LSU this can be minimised by planning activities with times of more noise in mind, and by the use of curtains or blinds.

If two teachers are functioning in the same room, the absorption of sound is crucial. Using carpeting and acoustic tiles on the ceiling and an acoustic screen will reduce the problem considerably. In addition, the behaviour of the pupils will be better in a quiet room rather than in an echoing room.

Some LSU staff find the use of soft background music helpful to create a calm atmosphere.

Furniture

If new furniture can be purchased, ensure that the LSU gets:

- light, comfortable but sturdy chairs, possibly stackable to give greater flexibility
- tables and working spaces that match the height of chairs for the learners (an expensive alternative is to have adjustable chairs so that they can be adjusted to the right height for each learner – preferable for both writing and using computers).

The arrangement of seating indicates the roles of teachers and learners. Serried rows of chairs indicates the teacher is to dominate; a circle implies more equality; a horseshoe with a chair in the gap is somewhere between the previous two. Different arrangements will be needed according to the learning activities taking place.

Heating and humidity

The room's heating from solar gain and from radiators and other systems can affect the behaviour and attention span of learners. Any division of the room should take into account the heat sources, and thermostatic controls could be installed if not present already. Adequate ventilation such as opening windows or louvres is essential to control the humidity. Using computers or audio-visual aids will raise the ambient temperature.

Lighting

Lighting needs to be adequate but not overly bright. Many LSUs are fitted with low glare rather than fluorescent lighting, and this can help to minimise the effects of bright and flickering lights. A room originally designed as a formal classroom may have extra lighting at one end. If computers are to be used it may be better to have these at the opposite end.

Too much glare from the windows can be a distraction. Venetian-type blinds give more control on light and solar gain.

Visual environment and colour

The use of pupils' work to decorate the room and celebrate success is essential. Display areas can be on the wall and the dividing screen. Proper display boards enhance the professional appearance and make the putting up and taking down of displays easier.

Some colours such as greens and light blues are considered calming, whereas bright colours such as reds and oranges have the opposite effect, enhancing the activities of a group that may already be over-active! Carpeting is better in a darker colour or with a lot of patterning to hide any spills, etc.

Computer links

It is very helpful if the LSU can be fitted with adequate computer facilities that are connected to the school network. This enables easier access to curriculum-based work, and enables pupils to continue to work on assignments already started in other lessons.

Because power points and network links may be in the wrong places with the re-organised room layout, it may be necessary to incorporate a false floor. In this case carpeting will be essential to prevent resonance from the space below.

Staffing

Ideally there are always two people working in an LSU, because this allows much greater flexibility of provision and opportunities for re-integration support and observations prior to interventions without the unit having to close for weeks on end. However, many units function very effectively with one very dedicated member of staff, who tries to be all things to all people and constantly feels as if they cannot do the job they would like to do. In many schools the LSU manager retains some teaching commitment in the mainstream school. The teaching of mainstream groups enables other staff to see their colleague working with larger groups as well as small groups and also enables the manager to keep in touch with mainstream classroom teaching. The majority of managers with whom I have worked are happy with this arrangement. However a word of caution is needed, because the balance has to be kept. The manager should not be used to replace unfilled positions until a subject specialist can be found. Managers may feel that their work in the LSU is undervalued and pupils can feel let down and unsupported. To counterbalance the LSU manager teaching some mainstream lessons, other members of staff could teach some specialist lessons in the LSU.

LSU managers and staff need to be able to disseminate good practice in working with challenging pupils, and developing a structure where this training and development can occur as part of the work of the LSU is beneficial.

It is worth considering staffing combinations and computations!

Use of LSU space

- Do you want the LSU to function as a working space at all times?
- Is it going to be a space where small groups of pupils (not necessarily referred to the LSU) work with a variety of members of staff?
- Will groups referred to the LSU be taught by a variety of members of staff?

Timetabling of LSU staff

- Will time for observations, communication with other staff and supporting re-integration be timetabled for LSU staff?
- Will all available time be timetabled, or will there be a level of flexibility built into the timetable of LSU staff?
- Will support for pupils take place in the LSU, or in their classrooms, or a mixture of both?
- If a mixture, how will this be decided?

Discipline

Some LSUs have developed their own policies, including discipline policies. The danger of this approach is that it can become an on-site alternative school with its own structures and codes. If we want the LSU to be part of a whole school approach it would seem beneficial to adapt the school's existing policies to reflect the implementation of the LSU and then all provision within the school share the same ethos and policies. This does not mean that within the LSU pupils will not have reward and sanction systems, but these, too, need to be treated with care.

Many LSUs set up complicated behaviour modification programmes with extrinsic reward systems, often based on a token economy. Not surprisingly this works well when pupils are in the LSU but fails when they are either re-integrating or attending mainstream lessons as well as attending the LSU. The problem with applying a behaviour modification programme without understanding the underlying psychology is that when it appears to fail the reasons are unclear.

The basic assumptions underlying a behavioural approach (from which behaviour modification programmes are derived) to teaching include:

- a concern with the observable

- behaviour is learned

- learning means changes in behaviour

- changes in behaviour are governed by the 'law of effect' (whether a behaviour is repeated depends on the consequences following it)

- behaviours are governed by the contexts in which they occur.

(Wheldall and Merrett 1984.)

If behaviour occurs because of its relation to antecedents and consequences, then changing the consequences or the antecedent events (or both) would change the behaviour. However, this change may be very context specific. For example, changing the responses of both teacher and pupil in Maths will not necessarily improve relations in Science, where the teacher has a different approach and the application would also need to be different. Burland (1984) notes that a token economy (one form of behaviour modification) works best in a closed community, such as a residential special school, because 'reinforcement can be more easily controlled and used effectively to change behaviour' (Burland 1984: 119).

This need for reinforcement to be tightly controlled is a problem in a mainstream secondary school, where teaching styles and expectations vary considerably from lesson to lesson. In addition, if we take a pupil in a school context there may be many influences on whether the reward for that behaviour (and therefore whether it gains a reinforcer for repetition in that context) is obvious or observable. Possible influences and reinforcers could include peers, teachers, parents, siblings, self-concept and the previous lesson. The antecedents to an initial encounter may be nothing to do with the present context, and although the consequence of this encounter influences subsequent encounters, it may demand much more in-depth unravelling than a simple 'law of effect'.

This example alone illustrates why it is important to ensure that the LSU is part of a whole school approach and not a separate entity.

Linked units

Linked units, or units which have pupils accessing them from more than one school, have particular problems of their own. Most of the primary LSUs (PLSUs) have been set up on this model and one of the case studies explored in Chapter 5 is how one PLSU has developed a linked unit model. Some secondary units also use this model.

It is worth briefly highlighting some additional issues for units which, although based in one school, also offer support for one or more other schools. In many respects the idea of a unit shared between several schools has advantages. The development of supportive communities around groups of schools offers a wealth of opportunities for sharing expertise and resources to meet the needs of individual pupils. In practice the process of setting up a shared unit needs to be well managed, and time and effort need to go into maintaining communications and a shared ethos for the running of the unit and the support it offers pupils. The steering group for these units is often a pivotal element of this communication framework.

Setting up the unit

All the school partners need to agree:

- the composition of the steering group
- the structure of access to the unit
- an overview of the curriculum offered
- referral procedures
- reporting guidelines, etc.

Although it is unlikely that all aspects of the provision will be 'right first time', if all the participants are in agreement initially then agreeing changes later will be easier.

If each school is to have a different amount of access this should be agreed in the initial stages and regularly reviewed.

Opportunities for staff from partner schools to visit the unit both before and after it starts to function are a useful way of making everyone feel part of the project. The professional relationship between the manager and the other staff in the unit is essential in developing policy and delivering practice. It is important that all staff feel informed about partner schools.

Referral procedures

These need to be agreed by all parties, but the LSU manager will need to think through what information he/she will need to work with pupils from a different school. In the first instance visits to the partner schools will be essential for the LSU manager to familiarise him/herself with differences in expectations, routines and procedures of the partner schools. The target setting and strategies worked on with pupils will be informed by these visits.

If it is possible for observations of referred pupils to take place, useful insights can be gained by staff from the LSU. It is also helpful if LSU staff can meet with pupils in their own school at some point prior to the placement. This helps to make clear links for the pupil.

Discipline

Discipline procedures for linked units may be different and this needs to be agreed by all the schools involved. Acceptable codes of behaviour for the unit should be clarified, and would generally follow the school's behaviour policy. In this instance we have policies of several schools, and while it is unlikely that they will be vastly different clarity needs to be sought. In addition, it is worth having a clear procedure about what will happen in the event of the pupil exhibiting unacceptable behaviour in either setting. Communication of incidents needs to be rapid and clear.

Logistics

There are a number of basic logistical issues that need to clarified:

- It is important to clarify for all concerned how pupils are going to get to and from the unit.

- If access is for full days this may be less problematic, but many units may offer sessions (these problems are not insurmountable but careful thought at the outset can prevent later worries).

- It is important that all pupils attending the unit are receiving the same kind of programme and that there are not disparities for linked schools.

- Times of the school day and procedures for break and lunchtime in each partner school will need to be clarified. If the timings in the LSU are to be different this will need to be agreed.

- Uniform is also an issue to consider. In most units the pupils will continue to wear the uniform of their own school, but this needs to be agreed.

Working with parents/carers

Working with parents/carers needs to be carefully considered:

- Parents/carers may be more tentative about their child spending time in the LSU if it is based in another school.

- The management of pupils' attending two different sites and pupils' individual needs should be planned.

- Parents/carers need to visit the LSU and be clear about logistics, for example how their child will get to the unit and back if this is on a sessional basis (see above).

References

Ajmal, Y. and Rees, I. (2001) *Solutions in Schools: Creative Applications of Solution Focused Brief Thinking with Young People and Adults*. London: BT Press.

Barrow, G. (2002) *Delivering Effective Behaviour Support*. London: David Fulton Publishers.

Barrow, G., Howard, P. and Hrekow, P. (2001) *Learning Support Units: A practical guide to setting up and developing in-school provision*. London: Dreyfus Training and Development Ltd.

Bennathan, M. and Boxall, M. (1998) *The Boxall Profile: A guide to effective intervention in the education of pupils with emotional and behavioural difficulties*. Maidstone: AWCEBD.

Burland, R. (1984) 'Behaviourism in the closed community: The token economy and performance contracting' in D. Fontana (ed.) *Behaviourism and Learning Theory in Education*. Monograph Series No. 1. Edinburgh: Scottish Academic Press.

Centre for Studies in Inclusive Education (CSIE) (2000) *Index for Inclusion: Developing Learning and Participation in Schools*. Bristol/London: CSIE/DfEE.

Cooper, P., Smith, C.J. and Upton, G. (1994) *Emotional and Behavioural Difficulties: Theory to Practice*. London: Routledge.

Cooper, P., Drummond, M.J., Hart, S., Lovey, J. and McLaughlin, C. (2000) *Positive Alternatives to Exclusion*. London and New York: David Fulton Publishers.

Daniels, H., Visser, J., Cole, T. and de Reybekill, N. (1998) *Emotional and Behavioural Difficulties in Mainstream Schools* (DfEE Research Report RR90). London: The Stationery Office.

DfEE (1999a) *Social Inclusion: Pupil Support* (Circular 10/99). London: The Stationery Office.

DfEE (1999b) *Excellence in Cities*. London: The Stationery Office.

DfES (2002a) *Guidance for Establishing and Managing LSUs*. London: The Stationery Office.

DfES (2002b) *An Audit Instrument for LSUs*. London: The Stationery Office.

DfES (2002c) *Good Practice Guidelines for Learning Support Units*. London: The Stationery Office.

DfES (2002d) *Audit Tool for Learning Mentors*. London: The Stationery Office.

DfES (2003) *Key Stage 3 Behaviour and Attendance Review*. London: The Stationery Office.

Dwivedi, K.N. (ed.) (1993) *Group Work with Children and Adolescents: A Handbook*. London: Jessica Kingsley Publishers.

Hallam, S. and Castle, F. (1999) *Evaluation of the Behaviour and Discipline Pilot Projects (1996–99) Supported under the Standards Fund Programme* (DfEE Research Report RR163). London: The Stationery Office.

Harris, D. and Bell, C. (1986) *Evaluating and Assessing for Learning*. London: Kogan Page.

Hill, F. and Parsons, L. (2000) *Teamwork in the Management of Emotional and Behavioural Difficulties*. London: David Fulton Publishers.

Jolly, M. and McNamara, E. (1992) *Towards Better Behaviour*. Ainsdale, Merseyside: Self-published.

Knight, B.A. (1992) 'The role of the student in mainstreaming' *Support for Learning* 7(4): 163–5.

Maines, B. and Robinson, G. (1988) *B/G-STEEM: A Self-esteem Scale with Locus of Control Items*. Bristol: Lame Duck Enterprises.

McSherry, J. (2001) *Challenging Behaviours in Mainstream Schools: Practical Strategies for Effective Intervention and Re-integration*. London: David Fulton Publishers.

Ofsted (2002) *New Developments in the Secondary Curriculum*. London: Ofsted.

Ofsted (2003) *Excellence in Cities and Education Action Zones: Management and Impact*. London: Ofsted.

Rhodes, J. and Ajmal, Y. (1995) *Solution Focused Thinking in Schools: Behaviour, Reading and Organisation*. London: BT Press.

Riley, K.A. and Rustique-Forrester, E. (2002) *Working with Disaffected Students*. London: Paul Chapman Publishing.

Tessmer, M. and Harris, D. (1992) *Analysing the Instructional Setting: Environmental Analysis*. London: Kogan Page.

Wheldall, K. and Merrett, F. (1984) 'The behavioural approach to classroom management' in D. Fontana (ed.) *Behaviourism and Learning Theory in Education*. Monograph Series No. 1. Edinburgh: Scottish Academic Press.

Index